Five Questions
That
Change Everything

D1710959

Five Questions
That
Change Everything

Life Lessons at Work

John Scherer

Word Keepers, Inc.
Published by Bibliocast
Fort Collins, Colorado

Word Keepers, Inc.
Bibliocast/Sat Nam Imprints/Imagine Books/Hawk's Cry Publications

Books are available at specialty quantity discounts for bulk purchases for sales promotions, premiums, fund-raising, and educational needs.
For details contact:
Tel. 970.225.8058
Fax 877.445.1007
www.wordkeepersinc.com

Copyright © 2009 by John Scherer

All rights reserved. This book, or parts thereof, may not be reproduced in any form without permission from publisher.

Interior and Cover Design: onedesign

Library of Congress Cataloging-in-Publication Data
Scherer, John
Five questions that change everything: life lessons at work/
John Scherer
    P.cm.
    Includes bibliographical references.
ISBN – 13: 978-0-9795315-2-1
ISBN – 10: 0-9795315-2-7
1. Personal growth – Problems, situations, contemplations, exercises, etc. 2. Self-actualization (Psychology)—Problems, exercises, etc. 3. Leadership in business – management, training, life lessons at work, exercises, etc. 4. Spirituality (Metaphysics)—Creative problem solving through awareness of signals and symbols in life relationships, etc.
I. Title
Printed in the United States of America
10 9 8 7 6 5 4 3 2 1

Dedicated . . .

to Daya, Barb, and Cath . . .
teachers on my path.

Applause . . .

A few years ago, I had the opportunity to observe a tradition at Boston College. It was a free, elective weekend called Halftime. BC students traditionally attend during their sophomore or junior year for a chance to step away from campus to reflect on where they have been, where they are, and where they are going. It's all about journeys, callings, and decisions. The centerpiece focuses on three questions: What gives you joy? What are you good at? And, does anyone need you to do it?

I found myself yearning for my own Halftime... for questions of depth and significance that would provoke answers to both the mundane and the magnificent potential we all still have... for questions that would provoke, prod, and produce a powerful response. And just imagine– a retreat just to answer questions! Not easy to come by in our 24/7, crazy, busy life.

You hold in your hand the answer to my yearning: five powerful questions that expand from my observations of youth into the richness of an adult world. Best of all, the NOW of our everyday life becomes the college for mining the gems of our individual souls. As the Zen master said, "Wherever you go, there you are." We carry within the key to improving relationships, living more authentically, and transforming our lives. The questions posed by this book will turn the key. What more could any self-explorer want?

—Eileen McDargh, CSP, CPAE, author, *Gifts from the Mountain: Simple Truths for Life's Complexities; Talk Ain't Cheap–It's Priceless,* and *Work for a Living and Still be Free to Live*

Foreword

by Elisabet Sahtouris, PhD

You are on the leading edge of evolution every day of your life, like it or not. Everything you experience, feel, think, and do is important to the whole community of Life. You are also meant to enjoy life deeply. That is your birthright, but it will not simply be handed to you; you must claim it. John Scherer has claimed it by learning from *whatever happens* in adversity as in good times. He has earned his stripes as a very good guide for others.

Whether John's newsletter comes to my mailbox from Kenya, where he has taken business managers to lay water pipe with the Merrueshi community of the Maasai while learning sound business principles from them, or from Poland, where he is bringing new practices of self-development and intrapreneurship to working people whose creativity was so long suppressed, his stories are lit up by the kind of genuinely transformative heart and spirit we so need in everyone's workplace, all over the world, and that we *can* have there.

I have loved all the good stories of transformation in this book, and my favorite is this one, for which the background is John's favorite phrase: *Remember, you don't need to* change *yourself; you need to* become *yourself—and that changes everything.*

> As one manager/engineer said recently at a seminar, *"Becoming myself?! What a bunch of California hot tub bullshit. Let's just dance around a candle and sing Kum Baya...."* That was on Day 1. You should have seen him on Day 4, emotionally talking excitedly about his new self-awareness and commitment to go back to his home and work, bringing all he now knew he could be. *"I can't wait to unleash myself back there!"*

This little story alone is testimony that this book has something for even the biggest skeptic. That manager/engineer discovered how to mine the deep riches of himself. As John teaches:

> There is a way to take even the worst
> experience of your life and find the upside,
> and vice versa. When you can generate
> an open spirit of inquiry regarding
> what happens to you, every experience
> becomes an opportunity for growth and
> development—and maximum contribution
> to others and to life.

The work of this book may not be easy, but it will be fascinating enough to keep you going as you learn to explore even your darkest shadows and mine them for gold. Think of the benefits to you if you can genuinely face the most challenging people in your life as valuable teachers who can help you transform yourself into your finest authenticity and fullest self- expression.

You might ask, why would an evolution biologist such as myself get excited about a book on life lessons at work, whose author characterizes it, furthermore, as being about "learning to learn from experience"? Where is the connection to our evolution as a human species?

The answer is really quite simple: All of biological evolution, including human evolution, is, from my vantage point, precisely about "life lessons at work" and "learning to learn from experience." To make this real for you, let's look briefly at how this can be. It is an important context for everything this book has to offer you—literally, the evolution of a whole new life you never dreamed possible, not just for yourself, but, as an added benefit, for our whole human family.

Although I was taught science as mechanistic reductionism in which all life is seen as blindly evolving mechanism, I eventually came to see Nature as arising within cosmic consciousness as a vast co-creative enterprise. Cosmic intelligence, from this perspective, now shared by ever more scientists, interacts with itself by individuating into a myriad of players from subatomic particles to the greatest galaxies. The most fascinatingly complex life forms, subject to influences from above as from below, seem to generate themselves literally halfway between the macrocosm and the microcosm, exactly where we are as humans.

"Learning to learn from experience" is the way of Nature. Evolution is no more about bits and pieces of chemistry coming together by accident and being selected by blind mechanical processes than are the computer assemblies without which today's world of work could not exist.

Our stunningly beautiful Earth has evolved the most amazing patterns of life for about four billion years now. Her natural economy has been a learning economy from which we, its latest players, have much to learn ourselves. From the time of our most ancient bacterial forebears, who had the planet to themselves for half its life, Earth's creatures have been learning to shift from the youthful species exuberance that begets creative invention and hostile competition to the mature discovery that cooperation has even greater advantages. That seems to be Nature's key learning process, the one by which countless surviving species have been transformed: the discovery that it is cheaper (more energy efficient) and far more secure to make friends of enemies than to outcompete or kill them. Species after species has learned this, transforming Type I ecosystems populated by immature species in hostile competition into Type III ecosystems characterized by their tightly woven inter-species collaborations.

Ancient Greeks, who invented the science that eventually evolved into ours, named it *Philos Sophias,* meaning 'love of wisdom', because the purpose of science, for them, was the study of Nature to find guidance in human affairs. This was precisely my purpose in becoming a scientist, though I soon discovered that natural science rooted in philosophy had been transformed into a practical science largely serving competitive marketplace purposes in a consumer society. That brings me now to 'life lessons at work.'

Just as Nature's economy is about making a living by transforming resources into useful products and services that are exchanged, distributed, consumed and/or recycled, so are the human economies in which most of us are employed. Further, Nature's economy is a complex living system; just so, all our businesses are made up of people and are therefore living systems. Yet the vast majority of human businesses do not function like healthy co-creative living systems, because they have been modeled on command-and-control machinery. Those few that have consciously reorganized themselves as living systems are now swimming upstream against the norm, often with great difficulty, and that just should not be, need not be, and must not continue to be.* It is high time to transform every workplace into a living system that is a great place to be—and it starts with the individual in relationship to others.

John Scherer asks us: *Do you find it hard to imagine your workplace as a really exciting and fun place to be?* Far too many people spend the week looking forward to weekend release from work, wondering whether life is only about showing up on time day after day, year after year, settling into your assigned place and doing your assigned work until liberated long enough to catch your breath before the cycle begins again.

---

* Sahtouris, E. "The Biology of Business: New Laws of Nature Reveal a Better Way for Business," Parts I and II, Perspectives on Business and Global Change, World Business Academy journal, Vol. 19, Nos. 3, 4, Sept. 2005 .
Link at www.sahtouris.com under Articles.

The good news is that when John turns your workplace into your 'school of life' everything changes and the fun begins. Odd as that may sound, since many of us watched the clock to Friday afternoon in schools as well, reframing your workplace as a context different from the one you have seen it to be until now is the first step in freeing yourself of constraints, not in locking yourself up in another kind of prison. As he says, there are no exams, no grades, and you get to invent your own curriculum to foster your own preferred learning.

This new view of the workplace as an exciting, creative kind of school actually transforms it, the way I see it, into a fascinating improvisational stage play in which you are the lead actor because the whole drama centers on your own transformation. The surprise benefit is that others around you will transform in reaction to your own evolving dance with them. Thus the potential of this book is to transform the entire workplace into a vibrant living system of people learning from each other as they, in John's words, "turn what happens at work into spiritual/personal development practice.... Where we are headed is nothing less than the unleashing of the human spirit at work—starting with your own."

My view of evolution is that of cosmic consciousness manifesting as individual life forms. This means that human nature is fundamentally spirit having human experience, and so it makes complete sense to me when John says:

This homework is work that takes you home—home to who you truly are, to the deepest place within you, to that Self which already *is* a master at being you. It's hard work to peel back the layers that have covered over this vital center, this core essence of who you are.

Discover this book as a powerfully transformative adventure—an exciting exploration into the archeology of the complex being you have become, with a long-practiced guide at your side. As he leads you into the deepest shadows of yourself, he will also show you how to transform those shadows into light. The Five Questions are powerfully transformative. If you stay with the process guided by them, you *will* get clear and positive results not only for yourself, but for your family, friends, and your workplace itself. They will, in turn, radiate out to our whole human species, now on the brink of its maturity as a peacefully cooperative global family that can learn to live better, even on a hotter Earth. As you evolve from automatic living to authentic living, you will, in John's words, get to "the Sweet Spot, the Zone, ... you will experience a kind of ecstasy, a joy, a sense of excitement and being on your 'edge.'" You will "go for *Tov!*" And as you do, you will become a beacon of light that others want to follow.

Elisabet Sahtouris, PhD, is an evolution biologist and futurist, author of *EarthDance: Living Systems in Evolution* and *A Walk Through Time: From Stardust to Us.*
Her website is www.sahtouris.com.

Turning Moments at Work into Lessons for Life

Everyone gets the experience; some get the lesson.

~ T.S. Eliot

I magine two people going to work every day, side by side, having virtually the same things happening around them. One goes home, upset yet again, blaming colleagues or himself, not having learned a thing—about who he is, about his relationships with others, or about life. The other person goes home more clearly on the path to a significant insight, or even transformation, using what happened that day to learn and grow.

What makes the difference? It has to do with attitude, the way each of those people approached his or her experiences during the day. It's simple, really. It only requires that you *seek a lesson in the experience*. The more you want that lesson, the more likely it is to happen. You will find what you seek.

Stuff Happens

You've seen the bumper sticker. In fact, you could see life itself as just a lot of stuff happening. All the time. Every day. A constant stream of moments, some positive, some negative. For most of us most of the time, these moments simply blend into a steady stream of indistinguishable experiences. Life becomes a blur of thinking about things, doing things, interspersed with occasional rest. We operate in a kind of trance, walking around, having a life, blissfully unconscious of a lot of what is going on, inside us and around us.

Every now and then, though, one of those moments stands out as different. The emotional needle jumps on the dial, and we become aware that 'something happened.' We might even realize that 'something *is happening right now.*' The moment might be more exciting or positive than usual, or more difficult or painful, but the result is that the trance is broken. It is in these moments when we are aware and alive that life can take on new meaning, or even a new direction. The FIVE QUESTIONS will show you how to turn these *moments* into profound personal and professional development *lessons.*

Let's get started.

As a human being, are you a finished product or a work in progress? Over the past few years, I have asked this question of thousands of people around the world and, as you might guess, *everyone* says, "Oh, I'm not 'there' yet; I'm a work in progress."

The next question I ask is, "Well, where do you do your progressing or developing?"

People respond with a variety of answers:

- ✧ reading a good self-help or leadership book
- ✧ going to personal or professional development seminars and workshops
- ✧ at my church, synagogue, mosque or spiritual development group
- ✧ sitting quietly alone or with close friends

These can all be wonderful places to be a work in progress. I know from personal experience, but I want you to consider another arena, one where you spend the vast majority of time during your lifetime: *your workplace*. Every day at work, you spend eight, ten, twelve hours in a *perfect* classroom for profound personal/spiritual development. As you will see, those people you work with—yes, those same ones—are the *perfect* faculty for what you are here to learn.

As you begin to work with the Five Questions, everything that happens to you on the job can become 'grist for the mill' of your spiritual development—and serve to maximize your contribution to the larger world. This will lead to greater purpose, power and peace. What more could you ask for?

The Workplace School Of Life

Every day you are at work, you are having literally thousands of moments, each one chock full of life-transforming potential.

The Workplace School of Life has a lot going for it:

⋄ This classroom is tuition-free. There are some costs associated with being in this school, but, as you will see, the cost is all internal, involving reflection and self-mastery.

⋄ Your faculty is always there—the ones you like and the ones you can't stand. In fact, as you will see, the ones you don't particularly like will be the most important ones for your development.

⋄ There are no grades, only your own inner critic. There is, however, continuous, real-time feedback happening all the time. The trick is to figure out what it means.

⋄ School is always in session and the lessons are always the right ones for you in that moment.

⋄ There are never any exams—only moment-by-moment tests. By the time we get to the final exam, it's too late!

Seva Is Sadhana

In Eastern traditions, there is a phrase that says it all. "Seva is sadhana." *Seva* is the job you do, the work you have, what you actually DO, such as washing dishes, talking on the phone, sitting in meetings, selling something. *Sadhana* is spiritual practice, that which deepens your self-awareness and contributes to your development into the human being you are capable of becoming. That saying is the gist of this book: how to turn what happens at work into spiritual/personal development practice

By this I do *not* mean your religion or theology or what you believe. You may or may not have a religion that means something to you. If you do, that religion is concerned with getting at what I am referring to here as 'spirit.' The founder of every religion knew *that* is where the real action is in human beings. What I mean by spirit is that which animates you. What has you get up in the morning? What is it that hums or beats at the center of who you are? That place from which you navigate your way through your moments. What I am talking about is beneath your mind, beneath anything that lives like a thought you can have. I mean that place from which those thoughts originate. That place to which you yearn to come home. That place.

What Does It Mean To Practice?

If you have ever learned to play a musical instrument, or a sport, or taken on any kind of new activity, you know what it means to practice. In this case, the mastery you are after comes with increased awareness of what is going on inside and outside. It means becoming more conscious and reflective, more curious, like a researcher: "Hmm, I wonder what that was all about? What's the lesson here?"

There's a catch, however. The thing you need to learn is very likely something you don't even know you need to learn. If you did, you'd be working on it. Remember the old adage: What you *know* is already working for you; what you *don't know* you are figuring out, but it's the stuff you *don't know you don't know* that's doing you in. How can you learn about things that you don't even know exist? It is possible. As Larry Wilson pointed out, there are definite stages in the process, however, based on an ancient Sufi saying:

> If someone is asleep and doesn't want to awaken, leave him alone.
>
> If someone is asleep but wants to wake, gently awaken him.
>
> If someone is awake but doesn't know, teach him.
>
> If someone is awake and knows, learn from him.

Are you awake or asleep in *your* workplace school? It doesn't matter, because—

Class Is Always In Session

If you start to see your entire life as a classroom for becoming who you are and what you are capable of being, then every meeting, phone call, interaction, decision, crisis, failure or success you have at work is an opportunity to learn and to develop yourself. Furthermore, those 'turkeys' you have to work with every day are your Faculty, carefully selected by the universe to be the perfect teachers for you, bringing up exactly what you need to be learning or developing next in your life.

Graduation

Unlike other classrooms you may have been in, however, this learning experience has no built-in grades, no evaluation by faculty, not even a graduation. There is only the learning itself. If that weren't strange and even troubling enough, the point of the learning you are doing here does not require that you change yourself in any way. Remember this crucial principle of the Five Questions: You don't need to *change* yourself; you need to *become* yourself. That changes everything.

The Assignment

Every learning experience from kindergarten to graduate school is designed around a set of objectives. If life is a classroom, then surely there must be objectives. I am convinced that, at birth, each of us was enrolled in The School of Life with a three-part assignment:

- ⬧ to continuously discover and completely develop into who we truly are,
- ⬧ to allow who we are to be fully expressed from moment to moment, and
- ⬧ to have that self-expression make meaningful and lasting contribution to the larger world.

Self-mastery

Those who understand much may be wise,
but those who understand themselves
are even wiser.
Those who are master over many may be powerful,
but those who have mastered themselves
are more powerful still.

~ Lao Tzu, 700 BCE

The kind of learning we humans are here to receive is not just about mastering a subject or a set of skills—the object of most classrooms. This classroom is more about the *self-mastery* to which Lao Tzu was referring: learning how to manage *internal* things like success, failure, fear, pride, confusion, and anger. There are skills to be learned here, but they are skills that assist you in processing what is happening to you, teasing out *lessons* from your *experiences*.

Homework That Takes You Home

If you decide to take on this program of self-mastery, *there will be homework.* Paradoxically, the work you will need to do has nothing to do with changing anything about yourself. It's exactly the opposite. *This homework is work that takes you home*—home to who you truly are, to the deepest place within you, to that Self which already *is* a master at being you. It's hard work to peel back the layers that have covered over this vital center, this core essence of who you are. The arena where your homework will take place is internal, and deep. Some would call it the soul.

Your homework will involve some of the most challenging self-development you have ever attempted. If you take it on, however, it will allow you to relax and enjoy your life, regardless of the circumstances, and know that you are doing and being *exactly* what you came here to do and be—and making the world a better place in the process. Whether or not you are aware of it, *this* is what you have been searching for, striving for, saving for, maybe even fighting for.

Why Five Questions? Why Not Five Answers?

Some might wonder how an approach based around *questions* could be of any value when what the world is seeking is *answers*.

First of all, questions are much more powerful than answers. As long as you are asking a question, you are open to input and discovery. The instant you find the answer, you stop looking; you shut down to new input. Answers eventually lead to rigidity. Rigidity leads to certainty. Certainty leads to stagnation. Stagnation leads to the need for fresh thinking and that requires asking the right questions.

The mind is basically a fast, smart computer designed to generate solutions for whatever question you put before it. Ask yourself, "Is this the right job/ life partner/body shape for me?" Your mind will scan its database and what it is seeing every day for possible answers to *that* question. The answers you receive will be in the form of some kind of assessment of your situation: "on the one hand ... but on the other hand ..." Ask another question, like, "What is present in this job/life partner/body shape that is fulfilling and full of potential?" and a completely different set of answers will show up. Garbage in, garbage out.

However, even having the right answers is apparently not enough. Aristotle was wrong. His belief was that "Those who *know* the good will *do* the good." Not today. At least not so you'd notice. Virtually everyone on the planet knows that smoking can kill you and that eating certain foods increases your chances of heart disease, yet both behaviors flourish. Research indicates that only about eight percent of people leaving their doctor's office actually go home and do what the doctor prescribed. It seems that even when we know what we should do, we often don't do it. Why?

Reason 1:   *Treating Symptoms*

Sometimes even your maximum effort to fix something fails to create sustained solutions because the 'answers' you applied were addressing *symptoms* and not root causes. You can change the way you dress, what you eat, how much exercise you get and so on, but as long as all of that is being done 'over the top' of the same core system of beliefs about yourself and the world, nothing of any lasting value will change. It's like papering over the old wallpaper or, to use an example that my colleague, Mark Yeoell, likes to apply from the environmental movement, "Make sure you are not working at 'the brown end of the pipe'!"

Root causes need to be addressed, not symptoms. What is 'upstream' or 'under the old wallpaper' of the issue for which you are seeking an answer? *That* is what needs to be discovered and fundamentally addressed. If you do not get at that deeper reality, whatever your issue is will continue to exist just beyond your reach, rising to the surface again and again as the same or another problem.

The answer you are seeking must be something that

  ⬦ addresses your fundamental issue, and
  ⬦ produces high-powered solutions, which
  ⬦ you actually carry out.

What you seek is an approach that creates the potential for *transformation*, a reality very different from that of merely *making a change*. *Change* can be accomplished by applying answers; *transformation* requires applying the right questions. The FIVE QUESTIONS are a great place to start.

Reason 2:   You Can't Really Change Yourself
Not only are most personal change efforts aimed at symptoms, they are also based on the premise that there

is something wrong with who you are now, the weight you carry now, the shape of your body now, the success you are having—or not having—now. Consider this: You couldn't have any other kind of attitude, relationships, weight, shape, or success, *given who you have been up to now*. If you want to create any kind of fundamentally different relationships, attitude, success, body shape, fulfillment or impact in your life, the secret is not to become someone else (*change*), but to become more fully who you are (*transformation*).

One more time: You don't need to *change* yourself— you couldn't anyway. You need to *become* yourself—and that will change everything. There is a Zen saying, "To the one wearing sandals, the whole world is leather." Change your 'sandals' and you change your world. Here's a real example:

The Woman Living Half A Life

Charlotte, a PhD child psychologist, came to the seminar with a vague sense of malaise, unusual for her, since she had long prided herself on being the eternal optimist and only experiencing the positive aspects of life. In our interaction, it became clear that she had been trained by her mother to 'always look for the silver lining.' Whenever illness or loss occurred, she was exhorted not to discuss it with neighbors—or even anyone in the family—out of fear that talking about it would validate its existence and give it energy. So she had been going through her life avoiding things like sadness, failure, loss, poverty, and laziness (a real no-no in her family).

At one point I said to her, "Charlotte, my good friend Mark Kelso, a gifted musician and songwriter, may have something for you here. He puts it this way:

HALF OF EVERYTHING

I want the up, but not the down; I want the smile, but not the frown.
I like the Yes, but not the No; don't want to stop; just want to go.
Don't want the darkness, just want the light; I want the day,
but not the night.
I want the honey, but not the sting; I want half of everything.

I like the fire, but not the burn; I want to know—don't want to learn.
I like Hello, but not Goodbye; I want to live, don't want to die.
I love to scratch, but not the itch; I love the goddess, but hate the bitch.
I want the honey, but not the sting; I want half of everything.

I like the half that makes me happy; I hate the part that makes me sad.
I love the gorgeous, the sweet and good; I hate the ugly, the bitter, and bad.
I like the pleasure and hate the pain; I worship the sun and shun the rain.
I want the honey, but not the sting; I want half of everything.

Courtesy of Mark Kelso ©1995 Mark Kelso, Muddy Angel Music

"Can you see," I challenged her, "how much energy you've been expending in a futile attempt to live half a life?! You are constantly having to sort, to eliminate large chunks of reality: 'I'll let *this* in, but not *that*.' What if you simply embraced all of life—and all of who you are, regardless of whether it seemed initially to be positive?"

After some minutes of intense interaction, Charlotte relaxed into acceptance of a particularly 'negative' aspect of her life: her rage. She saw what she had been missing, saw how much energy she had been expending in a futile attempt to keep her anger at bay, saw how okay it was to be a person who occasionally got angry. Through tears of relief and exultation, she blurted, "No wonder I've been exhausted and unhappy, and felt so ineffective!"

Charlotte, like each one of us, is operating with a powerful picture of herself: how she (and the world) is supposed to be. As you will see, that picture, given to you in childhood, is incomplete and woefully out of date. There are important aspects of who you are right now that you need to look squarely in the eye and get to know and accept as important parts of your reality. If you live in Chicago and you are planning a trip from there to Los Angeles, *you have to start in Chicago.* Every transformation begins with you standing completely, even gratefully, in the current space you occupy, exactly as it is.

For reasons you will learn, as humans, we have a tendency to 'throw the baby out with the bathwater,' trying to be only the 'good' or 'positive' side of who we are, relegating other, bad or negative or less acceptable aspects to the trash heap, denying to ourselves and those around us that anything like *that* could possibly be in us. You will find that your transformation will not come from polishing your (positive) act, but from rescuing and resurrecting a handful of discarded qualities. In Chapter Eleven, I will show you how to take these rejected 'shadow' attributes and turn them into 'stretches' for transforming your life, and thereby, your world.

New Water From The Old Well

As you now see, the difference between 'changing' something and 'transforming' it is that changing implies *replacing,* or in some way *negating*, what is there now. Transformation, on the other hand, implies reaching deep within what is there now to find the seeds for a new shape, a new reality. It is more like the true meaning of *education*: from its Latin root *e-ducare,* to draw out, as in drawing water out of a well. *You can think of the kind of transformation described here as drawing new water out of your old well—by going deeper than you ever dipped before.* The way to get your bucket deeper into your well is by taking on powerful questions, instead of jumping at attractive-looking answers. When you wrestle with these five life-changing questions, everything will shift inside and around you, starting with your understanding of who you are.

Ready To Go?

If you are ready, let's explore another way to live—and work. Perhaps you have a recurring thought that your life could—and should—be more than it is, that it just isn't adding up to what you always thought it would be. When you look beneath all the busyness of your day, is your soul joyful, expanded, and alive? Or is the drone of life numbing your heart and its yearnings? Do you find yourself hoping that God—or the universe, or someone or something, or a new job or a new boss—will show up and things will change?

If any of these are so for you, then you are going to love where we are headed.

The simple act of stepping on this new/old path—even though you may not know where it is going—will feel like you have come upon some fascinating new thing that just might bring you what you are searching for. In the process, it will also unleash you into greater impact beyond yourself, out there in the larger world, which is waiting eagerly for you to show up fully as you are.

The approach is actually very simple. Not easy, but simple. Here it is.

Come Home To Yourself

Come home to your Self. Not the little self, the one that worries all the time, and tries hard to impress people and keep up the illusion of safety and control. I'm talking about coming home to the *huge* Self, the one that truly *lives* and loves and knows why it's here, and can't wait for the next sunrise. The one that yearns to encounter the next challenging person or situation, because of what will be learned in that fire. Your true Self, your higher or deeper Self, the one that understands where your interpretation of this life comes from, that knows how to shift shapes and shift states. The one that has not given in to the default trances of this world's concepts about life.

Let's take a walk together and discover—or re-discover—*that* path of turning work—and life itself—into spiritual development. When you were born, you were a master of that way of learning. In fact, it was all you knew how to do at first. You were a *learning being,* designed to grow and develop and discover yourself and the world in every moment of every day.

The more you learn about this approach, the more you will see that some of the people you bump into occasionally wander on this path, too, even if how they go about it looks very different. All spiritual paths and religions are about this 'way' that seems so hard for us humans to travel. Perhaps you have tried one or more of these approaches yourself. It's sad, but, in their efforts to help people get there, these paths often become victims of the very trances they want to break. Rather than staying open to the life-changing *questions* their founders—who were all master learners—wrestled with, the followers of those enlightened ones have settled into a set of *answers*, growing rigidly certain, losing touch with the developmental process of life. Born to be *learners*, most of us have turned into *knowers*. The work-in-progress we believe ourselves to be has stopped progressing, and every day feels like more of the same only different.

As you will see, taking on the FIVE QUESTIONS will keep you fresh, vital, engaged, and alive. Living inside a world of answers—even good ones—will eventually lead to feelings of stagnation, helplessness, and anxiety—the opposites of purpose, power, and peace.

So, let's walk a while, and let me show you how to turn anything and everything that happens to you into a *spiritual development moment,* a flash of awareness that deepens and expands you more fully into your huge Self, and maximizes your contribution to others, and to life itself.

I'll say it again: You don't need to *change* yourself. You need to *come home* to your Self. That will change everything.

Where we are headed is nothing less than the unleashing of the human spirit at work—starting with your own.

Question 1: What confronts me?

Q1

Chapter One

Facing the Tiger

This first of the FIVE QUESTIONS asks you to look at your life at work and pick out a recent moment that still has some strong emotional or mental energy associated with it. It could be a positive or a negative experience, but I want you to start working with one that you would like to have avoided if you could have. Think of a situation that is confronting you and has you thinking, "I sure wish *that* hadn't happened!" Transforming one of *those* moments has truly transformative potential. As you will see, paradoxically it is actually a little easier to work with what you would see as a negative experience. There seems to be more juice there, and the lessons you are seeking are closer to the surface. Not to worry, you will soon see the positive potential in the moment you choose.

How would you *name* that moment? As Toronto-based

colleague Sandy Wise says, it all starts with naming what is happening. Give what is confronting you a handle. Call it something. The name you give it will almost certainly change as you go through the FIVE QUESTIONS, but you must start by saying in words what it is that confronts you.

On Running From A Tiger

Think of what you are doing as facing the tiger. If you lived and worked in the part of the world where tigers live, and a tiger were to come upon you suddenly, what would be your first (human) instinct? Run! Yes, run! However, if you do turn away and run, six million years of evolutionary training kicks in. The tiger's eyes see a small, slow figure running away, as my colleague, Mark Yeoell, says, "The yummy one with the crunchy center." The tiger's brain registers, "Lunch!" with great delight. Then the tiger runs you down and kills you, either eating you immediately or saving you for later.

Tigers are hard-wired to chase a small, slow, pudgy figure running away. Are you kidding? They can't stop themselves. If you have a kitten, and you drag a string in front of it ten times, how many times will the kitten jump on the string? Ten times out of ten. Chasing a figure running away is hard-wired into the tiger's—and all felines'—operating system.

The bottom line: if you run away from a tiger, your chances of survival are essentially zero. However, the people who live amongst tigers say that if you turn and *face* the tiger, maybe not. Now, let's be clear, it may still eat you! This is not some magic story here, but the tiger will stop for a moment and think about what it wants to do. So, if you face the tiger, your chances of survival are somewhat greater than zero. In the simple act of turning and *confronting* the tiger, you have created not a guarantee but a *possibility*, a possibility that wasn't there before. That's all, just a chance, but it's a chance for a different outcome, which is significantly better than the alternative.

A 'tiger' is often a conversation you know you need to have, or a situation you know you need to turn and face, people with whom you need to speak about something bothering you or affecting your work team, organization, family, or friendship. The alternative is to continue to walk—or run—away from them, and hope they don't chase you. But consider this: *If you are not facing one of your tigers, it's already eating you.* Running away from an issue actually makes it loom more powerful than it often is.

Where do you sense the presence of a tiger in your life?

- ⬦ work
- ⬦ family/loved ones
- ⬦ relationships/friends
- ⬦ health and well being
- ⬦ personal/spiritual development
- ⬦ finances
- ⬦ community and larger world

Crisis: *A Choice Point*

You may never face an actual tiger, but the physiological and psychological response in your body, mind, and spirit when you have been confronted by any truly frightening situations in your life is exactly the same. Just think *conflict* or *crisis*. By the way, the original Greek word for crisis is the verb 'to choose or decide.' A crisis is simply a choice point. What do you do in those situations? There are five basic human responses to conflict. What is your pattern or sequence? Most people employ several that come in a familiar order. Which comes first for you? Then which one? What would be your Last Resort?

⋄ FIGHT—taking on the threat with the intention of beating or neutralizing it

⋄ FLIGHT—turning away, disengaging, and either walking or running in the other direction

⋄ FREEZE—standing very still, 'like a deer in the headlights,' in hopes that the threat will pass you by

⋄ FIGURE OUT—going into the mind to try to analyze what is happening, what the problem is, and what to do

⋄ FIX—attempting to solve or resolve the situation, eliminating the cause of the conflict or threat

A *Personal Example*

Typically, before developing the FIVE QUESTIONS approach, my first response to a conflict with someone I cared about, personally or professionally, was to FREEZE. "Oh, my God! How did I get here?!" Then my childhood training would kick in and I would think, "It's my fault. I must have done something wrong." Then, very quickly I would move into trying to FIGURE OUT what was happening and, as soon as possible FIX things. The startling insight I had when I saw my pattern, however, was that what I was trying to *figure out* and *fix* was not the problem or the cause, but the upset itself! All my energy went into trying to mollify *the other person's feelings toward me.* "What can I do to have them not be so mad at me?"

This pattern ended suddenly for me one afternoon in Hartford, Connecticut, when Carol, a client, good friend, and Senior VP at Aetna (my largest account at the time), was driving me to the airport after a one-day consultation with her leadership team. In our second year of working together, she had become a real champion of our work inside the company, having hired us to do several large projects in her division, and sending fifteen or twenty of her key managers through our Executive Development Intensive. After our session, as we were getting into the car, I noticed she was quieter than usual, but didn't think anything of it.

We made small talk as we turned onto I-84, with Carol driving and me in the passenger seat. Suddenly she turned toward me and began to shout, *"John Scherer! What the @#$% were you doing in there?! You embarrassed me in front of my people! You undercut everything I have been trying to do with them! I can't believe you did that to me! I'm inclined to not ever bring you in again!"*

My life passed before me. I froze. I could hardly breathe. My heart was pounding in my chest. I remember turning toward her in my seat, absolutely terrified. It all kicked in: first my childhood training ("Be the good boy"), then my terror ("Oh, my God, she's about to *fire* me!"). Here was my favorite client—and by then good friend and colleague—telling me we were finished. Practically, that also meant that fifty percent of our company's revenue was about to go out the window, and I had just hired three new people and signed a five-year lease on a new office suite, based in large part on continuing contracts with her and Aetna. Life, as I had known it, was over.

All this ran through my mind in a flash, and contributed to my complete inner collapse.

Then an amazing thing happened. *I let go.* I let go of our friendship, the contract with Aetna, my new office space, the people I had just hired, even the future of my fledgling business. Then I let go of my pride, as I confronted what felt like the real possibility of a shameful bankruptcy—or at least the drastic reduction of what we were doing in the world and how we were doing it. I recall sitting there, calmly, quietly, letting her hurt and anger come toward me. It was as if I were in the eye of a hurricane, with all kinds of turmoil swirling around me. I felt and gently discarded the urge to try to figure out what had happened and to explain and defend my actions. I just sat there, facing her, and 'holding the burn' as we say in yoga.

Eventually, her intensity faded, and by the time the half-hour ride to Bradley Airport was over, we were able to have a conversation about what had happened and where to go from there. As we drew into the parking lot, she turned to me, smiled warmly, and said, *"Thank you, John, for the way you handled this exchange. I wish my staff could do what you just did."*

On reflection, we both learned a lot from that experience, but what I discovered about facing the tiger has been part of my life ever since. *Facing is not fighting.* It is something else, and that's what taking on Question 1 is all about. *Running away* gives the issue or the other person energy *indirectly;* it makes it bigger in your mind. *Fighting* an issue or the other person gives them energy *directly.*

Facing it ... now that's another story.

The Scout Master And The Gunslinger*

Terry had been appointed to the Chief Operating Officer (COO) position of his insurance company by the outgoing CEO. The new guy didn't particularly like or respect Terry but was willing to honor the promise made by his predecessor. That made them professionally appropriate but wary colleagues. After two years of this, their organization was polarized from top to bottom around their unresolved conflicts of leadership style and values.

Terry was a 'gunslinger,' ready to jump into any opportunity that felt good to him and that showed signs of potential. Dale, his CEO boss, was just the opposite, a 'boy scout,' careful to not make a mistake, cautious about moving too fast, and nice to a fault—except when his irritation leaked out during staff meetings in sarcastic, put-down humor, which subordinates laughed away nervously. Both were actually Eagle Scouts, an award achieved by less than ten percent of all Scouts in the world. In fact, Dale had served as a national Boy Scout Leader, and his careful, detail-oriented style was

---

* This real-world example is a chapter in *Chicken Soup for the Soul at Work*, by Jack Canfield, Mark Victor Hansen, Maida Rogerson, Martin Rudde, and Tim Clauss (1996).

a positive role model for many young people. Terry, beloved by those who worked for him, was a people person with a warm, engaging, inspiring, motivating style, who saw the big picture and sought ways to involve people in that vision.

At the Leadership Development Intensive he attended, Terry had a chance to rehearse the Face-the-Tiger conversation he was thinking about having when he got back, speaking to an empty chair as if Dale were sitting there. After several minutes of increasingly direct discourse—Terry, moving back and forth between the two chairs, speaking first for himself, then for Dale (imagining what he might say), then himself, and so on—suddenly he stopped in mid-sentence with a look of complete surprise on his face. He told us what he was now seeing: The person who *should* be sitting in that empty chair, the person who *should* be receiving Terry's anger about his not being seen or respected or appreciated was not Dale, but *Terry's own father.* Terry had the life-altering insight that he was working out his stuff with his dad in his interactions with Dale. He recalled my quote: *"When you're hooked, you're history."* Emotionally hooked in virtually every conversation with Dale, Terry realized that he was viewing Dale through his own glasses, those lenses ground by his early training and his family history.

This insight enabled Terry to look at Dale *around* his glasses for a change, rather than *through* them. When he did, he saw that all he wanted from Dale was his approval, something Terry never got enough of from his own father. He saw how he was expecting

Dale to make up for something that was actually Terry's issue to resolve. Terry made a commitment to have a Face-the-Tiger conversation with Dale as soon as he could to share this insight and work out a new way of interacting—one that might ease the conflict and stress they were causing their entire organization.

As it so happened, on his way back home from his Intensive, Terry found himself "Just going by the office to check my e-mails," not expecting to meet anyone at 6:00 p.m. on a Friday evening. As he walked to his office, he noticed that the door to Dale's office was standing open, and Dale was there, at his desk! *"Oh, my gosh!"* Terry thought, as he told us later. *"He's here! Well, okay, buddy, you'd better go for it. There's no time like the present to face the tiger!"*

He went in, shared his insight, and asked for Dale to forgive him for expecting him to compensate for what he missed getting from his father. Terry initiated a conversation intending to dramatically shift the way they related to each other, especially in front of their people. Seeing how destructive his sarcasm and put-down humor was, Dale agreed not to use it on Terry anymore, admitting it was an indirect way of dealing with his extremely popular, but unpredictable COO. He also promised to let Terry in on financial discussions that had been off-limits up to then. For his part, Terry agreed to stop bad-mouthing Dale to his people, and to check certain decisions with Dale, ones that he knew Dale was nervous about.

Their open wound had started healing, and even people several levels below the rarified air of the executive floor could tell almost immediately that there was a new game in town, one without the rancor and sarcasm of the recent past. While Terry and Dale never became best friends, their relationship deepened enough to allow them to genuinely appreciate the amazing gifts each was contributing to the company's success. Their new respect for each other also allowed their people to agree or disagree with them on crucial decisions without being seen by the other party as disloyal. The result: better decisions, made with the focus on the problem to be solved, rather than on minimizing exposure to a counter-punch from the other side.

Chapter Two

Pinch, Crunch & Crisis Utilization

This next conceptual model or map will show you: why tigers are a built-in aspect of all healthy relationships, when a tiger is worth facing, how to get started, and what is likely to happen if you don't.

The Pinch Theory *

Every relationship, whether between individuals or groups of people, begins with a period of Gathering Data and Sharing and Clarifying Expectations. Rarely does someone walk up and say, "Hi, my name is John. I'd like to gather some data and share and clarify some expectations!" Nevertheless, that's exactly what's happening when people are starting to explore a relationship at home or at work, whether it's a job interview or a social event. "Hi, where are you from?

---

* First developed by John Sherwood and John Glidewell in 1969, it was called "Planned Re-Negotiation: A Norm-Setting OD Intervention." This current version is adapted from John J. Sherwood and John J. Scherer's "A Model for Couples: How Two Can Grow Together" from the *Journal for Small Group Behavior,* February, 1975.

What do you do?" etc. *What's going on here? Who is this other person? What can I expect from him? What does it look like she'll expect from me?* They're finding out about you and you're finding out about them. You're getting as clear as you can about expectations. This first stage is about *learning* or *discovery*.

The dilemma is that, in the early stages of the relationship, both sides are trying to look good. Both people are in what my colleague Ron Short, calls "the mating dance of the Watusi bird." Both of you have your feathers all fluffed up and are prancing around *trying to look like the best _____ (fill in the blank) possible*. This is not a bad thing, this is a human thing.

In trying to make a good impression, you don't say, "Oh by the way, under pressure, I yell a lot." Or, "When things get really bad, I'm probably going to miss work for several days." These kinds of things just don't come out. You don't talk about your down side; you emphasize the positive things. Plus, even if you wanted to, it is impossible to know, in advance, what you need to talk about. Things only come up later in the course of the relationship unfolding as it does.

Based on the information that does get exchanged, you start to have a sense of what the expectations are, and you are then able to move to the next phase: Role Clarity and Commitment. "Ah, now I see what it would mean to be director of marketing for this organization." "Now I see how it would be to be in a relationship with you." To the extent that the role feels comfortable, you then make a commitment. You go, "Yes! Okay. I'm in. I'm a part of this. Count me in."

The Pinch Theory

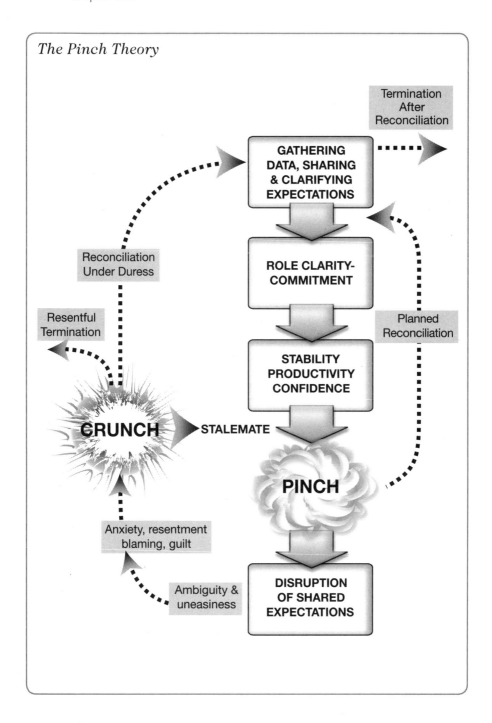

As soon as that commitment occurs, you are able to move to the next phase, which is Stability, Productivity, and Confidence. You could say the relationship 'works.' You can now work together, live together, whatever. There is a certain amount of stability here: *"Now, I have a sense of clarity about what is going to happen between us."* And some predictability: *"I think I can see what will happen when stuff comes up."* And confidence: *"I also have at least a little bit of confidence in how we are going to do together. You know, this just might work out."*

The Pinch

Right in the middle of that period of stability, productivity, confidence—someone is going to experience what we call a Pinch. A Pinch is a little thing that happens between you and another that bugs you. It is probably *not* something you talk about right away, but is something that, if it were to keep up, could become a problem.

What kinds of pinches occur in your workplace and home life? Little things like:

⋄ showing up late for meetings

⋄ missing deadlines

⋄ leaving coffee cups on people's desks

⋄ talking about people behind their backs

⋄ taking credit for what someone else did

⋄ not taking out the garbage after saying you would

⋄ leaving the toilet seat up/down

In our North American culture, are we trained to talk about Pinches or *not* to talk about them? Usually we don't talk about them. What are some reasons we give ourselves for not talking about Pinches?

- ⬥ It's no big deal.
- ⬥ It's my problem.
- ⬥ Don't create conflicts.
- ⬥ It probably won't happen again.
- ⬥ I'm sure they didn't mean it.
- ⬥ I don't want this thing to blow up.

The bottom line is that when a Pinch occurs you often say to yourself, "Oh well, let's just go back to work again."

Here's the key point: If you don't talk to the other person about what just happened, what do they learn? Nothing. In fact, as hard as it might be for you to believe, they might not even know that they *did* anything! I suppose it's possible that they are lying awake at night trying to think up ways to tick you off or mess up your life, but chances are they are just going along, doing what they do, being the way they are. As my Pop used to say, *"Son, everyone is just trying to get to the Post Office."*

Regardless of the other person's motivation, let's say you don't talk about what has happened. No information gets exchanged. Guess what happens next. The Pinch occurs again, and even again; and every time it happens, inside you, a little weight goes on a scale. Click, *"That's one."* Click, *"That's two."* Click, *"That's three."*

Then, after a certain number of times, depending on the issue, that scale tips over and you find yourself in a new situation which drops you down into that next box: *Disruption.* What is happening now is a very clear disruption of the expectations you had at the beginning. You say to yourself, *"Whoa, wait a second. This is not what I signed on for! This is not what I said 'Yes' to. I didn't know this was going to happen."* Something snaps, and you can no longer pretend it doesn't bug you. Now, it bugs you, and it throws you very predictably into the path to the left side of the Pinch Model, where there is usually a tremendous amount of *Ambiguity and Uneasiness.* You can be thinking, *"Wait a minute. If I can't trust him about _____, I wonder whether I can trust him about _____?!"*

The Crunch = Crisis

That very quickly moves you from a mere Pinch to what we call the Crunch, where lie Anxiety, Guilt ("I should have said something ..."), Anger, and Resentment. You are flat-out upset. Imagine the graphic dial on your music system that shows you how loud things are. When a Pinch occurs, your emotions just barely jiggle the little needle on the meter, but when you get to the Crunch point, that needle is slammed over into the red zone. It's on the peg.

The Crunch is actually a crisis. The word *crisis* comes from the Greek verb *krisein*, which means 'to chose or decide.' You are now at a choice point; you are going to have to do something. You can't take it—or fake it—anymore. What are your options?

The most popular choice is to do the same thing you did at the Pinch: "I don't want to make a bigger problem out of this, so let's just go back to work, let's get back to the way things were." We call that Premature Reconciliation. It's premature because there has been no conversation, no discussion of what happened. You just gut it out, suck it up, go back to work again. "One more time for the Gipper."

Okay, great, you're back to the way it was before the Crunch. Then what happens? The Pinch occurs again. And what do you say to yourself? *"Oh well. Here I am again. I still don't want to create a bigger problem."* This time, though, it doesn't take quite as many 'trigger' moments to put you at the Crunch point again. If the pattern continues, you go round and round and round in a big circle, *passing through* the period of Stability, Productivity, and Confidence. Pretty soon your relationship is in the tank and you can't get any work done with this person anymore. After a few trips into the Crunch, *fear*—which is always beneath *anger,* by the way—comes into play, driving out the confidence and stability that you had before.

After a few tries at Premature Reconciliation, you may be ready for another option. You may find yourself saying, *"I don't need to take this anymore. I'm out of here."* You spin off to the left there into what we call Resentful Termination. There are lots of ways to do this:

- ❖ You can arrange to get transferred.
- ❖ You can arrange to get promoted.
- ❖ You can arrange to get fired.
- ❖ If it's a personal relationship, you can pack and leave.
- ❖ You do whatever you need to do to get away from the scene.

Resentful Termination: *Leaving Mad And Dumb*

The problem with Resentful Termination is that when you leave that way, you leave Mad and Dumb. You take your anger and your ignorance with you. You may think you're leaving the bad stuff behind, but you are taking your unfinished business with you to the next marriage, the next job, the next relationship. Every time you went around that loop from Pinch to Crunch and didn't address the issue(s), a little lump of you-know-what went into a sack: plop, plop, plop. After a while you're carrying around a big gunny sack full of you-know-what, and you say, "I'm leaving. I'm not going to be around that stuff anymore."

Would that it were so. When you leave, what you don't realize is that you drag that sack with you to wherever you go next. The sack has a hook on it, and as you walk out the door, that hook grabs your belt and comes along for the ride. Ever hopeful that you've left all that you-know-what behind, you go to the next place, the next relationship, the next job. *"Hi, my name is John. I'd like to gather some data and share and clarify some expectations. Man, this is great! This isn't anything like that other place!"* Unbeknownst to you, that sack is right behind you. Then, one day in a meeting, somebody does something that ticks you off and that sack comes over your head and goes plop all over everybody in the room, and people say, *"What the heck was that all about? Two and two is adding up to six here."*

What happened was that all of your unfinished business just got dumped on these new people, whether or not it was rightfully theirs—like the angry person who goes home from the office and kicks the dog.

Let's say you don't want to split; you don't want to leave the job or the relationship because it's got a good pension plan, or you've got kids or a family to think about. What are you going to do? There is another option. It's really almost a *default* option, because most people spend at least some time in its clutches. Instead of your energy going 'up and out' in an expression of upset, it's the path that goes 'down and in.' We call it Stalemate. That's where you don't have the energy any more to try to make it work, and you don't want to leave, so you end up resigned to the situation. You end up stuck in the middle of things.

A lot of marriages and work partnerships hang out in this place. Walk into any bureaucratic organization with a lot of rules and regulations, with a lot of people that have been doing the same thing for years and years, and you may see this. It's as if 'the light's on, but there's nobody home.' In that particular relationship or organization everybody has given up. Nobody is trying anymore. They have 'resigned on the job' or 'resigned in the relationship.'

Fortunately, there's another option, or this map wouldn't be worth a thing. That path is to *go back up to the top, face the tiger, and talk about what is happening.* We call it Reconciliation Under Duress. Since that option is so scary for so many people, it usually only happens under duress, under pressure. Maybe the boss comes in and says, *"Look, you two get this figured out or else I'm going to figure it out for you."* Or if it is a home situation, your partner says, *"We are going to a counselor or I'm out of here."* The 'duress' part means that there is some kind of pressure brought to bear that makes you say, *"I guess I've got to face the tiger and talk about this."* It is truly ironic that "Let's talk about what's happening" is often the last resort.

If you take this path back up to the top, you usually start by saying something like, *"You know, the very first time you did _____, I should have said something to you about that. I apologize, I have to take responsibility for not saying anything; but, this is not working anymore. Can we talk about that?"* Then they say, "Yes" or "No," and you go from there. What's happening is that new data, new information, is entering the system. Based on that new information you begin to get a sense of new (shared) expectations. *"Oh, I get it. It doesn't work when we do that. How do we need to change?"* You negotiate back and forth until you get a new sense of Role Clarity. As soon as you get that new sense of Role Clarity, you create a new sense of Commitment to the relationship.

"Hey, this is working again!" That's why making up is so much fun. You have a face-the-tiger conversation with somebody, and all that energy that was spent going around and around avoiding everything can now be put into the relationship or the work again.

The Pinch: A Choice Point

So, the relationship 'works' again. Fantastic. What happens next? Another Pinch. Is there any way to be in a real, dynamic, mutually rewarding relationship at home or at work and *not* have Pinches? No. It's impossible. Because, if you are in any kind of professional or personal relationship with *anybody* where you need something from the other person on a regular basis, there are going to be Pinches. What is the likelihood that one hundred percent of the time—forever—you are going to be able to give that other person exactly what they need at exactly the right time and in exactly the right way? Or that they will give you what you need when you need it one hundred percent of the time? It's zero. Sooner or later a Pinch is going to occur.

You've Got Mail

In fact when the Pinch occurs, you ought to be grateful, even celebrate! Because the Pinch is telling you that there is something about your relationship that is out of date. There is something that needs to be made more real, more current. Some kind of learning needs to take place. Think of the Pinch as a kind of *gift,* an early warning radar. Like the icon on your computer inbox that says, *"You've got mail.* There is something here you just might want to check out."

That means when someone—anyone—walks up to you and says, "I've got a Pinch with you; can we talk about it?" the first words out of your mouth should be, "Thank you!" Can you see why? Because,

- ◇ you know they have thought about it for a while.
- ◇ it has taken some courage on their part to bring it up.
- ◇ they are saying the relationship is important enough to risk the conversation.

Chapter Three

Pay Now or Pay Later

When you and the person with whom you've reached a Pinch or Crunch point recognize and address the issue, you are in a position to resolve it. You have become aware, as the old motor oil commercial put it: "You can either pay now, or pay later." You are either going to pay a relatively small amount to put in a new oil filter, or, down the road, you are going to have to put in a new engine, or maybe even get a new car.

Making Pit Stops

Racecar drivers understand this principle. They know from experience that you can't drive a car two hundred miles an hour more than so many laps without making pit stops. They make two kinds of pit stops. One is when smoke is coming out of the back; but they also make pit stops every ten laps or so. Let's say they don't need gas. Why do they make those pit stops? Because they need to look at having to change tires, check for stuff that might be showing some wear. They know they have thousands of parts running really fast, really hard, and they *expect* certain things to need attention.

They don't get mad at the car when it comes into the pit for one of those planned stops. They know right where the hot spots are likely to be. They know that after so many minutes of running that fast, if something's going to happen it's liable to happen here, here, and here. They check, fix what needs attention, and then v-r-o-o-m, back out on the track again.

We, on the other hand, don't make pit stops in our most important relationships. What do we do? We get in our relationships and we 'drive' them round and round, real fast, under great pressure, never making pit stops, and then all of a sudden B-A-N-G! Things blow up, and we have to get another car/employee/partner.

We do maintenance on our cars and computers, but not with people and relationships. Isn't that ridiculous? The Pinch Theory says we should *plan* for Pinches, applying the principle called Planned Reconciliation. That means standing at the Pinch point or the Crunch point and saying, *"Thanks for telling me about what's happening. Let's talk about it."* Face the tiger, and go back up to the top to have a conversation.

The mutually healthy, vibrant relationship starts at the top and comes down into Commitment and then Stability, Productivity, and Confidence. When a Pinch occurs, as it inevitably will, you have a choice: you can let it slide and hope it doesn't happen again, or you can mention it right away—while your emotions are not running full out.

Termination After Reconciliation: Leaving Sad But Wiser

When you face the tiger and go back up to the top to have the Pinch or Crunch conversation, you do not have to leave a relationship Mad and Dumb. You might decide—after truly seeing *your* role in what happened, doing some deep exploring and weighing the long-term cost/benefit—that this relationship is just not going to work. When that other arrow at the top goes up and off to the right, we call it Termination after Reconciliation. When you leave from this place, you leave Sad but Wiser.

'Reconciliation' is a very interesting word. It comes to us from the Romans by way of the Greeks. *Dialasso* is the Greek word, and it means to be changed (*lasso*) through the center (*dia,* diameter), in the heart. To be reconciled to another person means to allow yourself to be changed, fundamentally changed, through your center. You could say transformed.

Can you see how Pinches with other people could become opportunities to learn something crucial about yourself and enhance your capability for living and working with greater purpose, power, and peace?

It is possible to get to the point where you've changed (*dialasso'd*) so much that you think, *"I just can't dialasso anymore. I have tried my best and this is not going to work. I realize now how I got into this situation. I see my role in getting to this place I don't like. I've learned some important things. The only path left is to go our separate ways."* You leave Sad but Wiser. It's not avoidance working here; it's wisdom working. Would you rather hire somebody that is coming off Mad and Dumb or Sad but Wiser? Would you rather start a relationship with somebody that is coming off Mad and Dumb or Sad but Wiser?

Yes, But ...

I can imagine what you are thinking at this point: "That's all well and good, John, but what if my life or business partner is not at the same place I am? What if they don't want to have a face-the-tiger conversation with me? What then?" Yes, believe me, I have heard this before—and been there myself a few times.

It's very unusual to have both people ready for this at the same time and for both to be at the same level of skill and/or commitment. One thing you can do is share this Pinch Theory with them. Don't talk just yet about the issue or Pinch *itself*, but, instead, talk about your desire to have a Pinch conversation as soon as they are ready and willing. Tell them the issue and your relationship is important to you.

Use A Third Party

The other suggestion is, anytime you get past the Disruption point and/or around to the Crunch, you really need to have what we call a Third Party be in the conversation with you. A committed listener, someone who is neutral about the issues and doesn't take sides—and is a pretty good communicator. It doesn't have to be a therapist or life coach (if it's at home) or a consultant (if it's at work), although that would be best in truly adversarial situations.

One crucial key in having a face-the-tiger conversation where you use the Pinch Theory, is this:

Do not go in with the goal of winning an argument or teaching the other person, but to *learn*—learning something about yourself and about the other person, about relationships and how to have one that works. More on exactly how to do that will be presented in Question 5: WHAT WILL UNLEASH ME?

When To Face The Tiger

How do you tell when a tiger is one that needs to be faced? If you confronted every Pinch that happened to you, you'd have little time left for anything else. The Pinch Theory gives us some clues about how to discern what deserves to be faced and what does not. Obviously, a Crunch must be dealt with. Whenever your 'needle is on the peg' and you're upset about something, that's a good indicator of an issue that needs to be confronted.

Here are four questions I have found helpful in sifting through all the stuff that happens, for determining when I must turn and face the tiger. These are questions worth asking yourself when you are not sure:

⋄ *How important is the* **relationship***?* If the Pinch is with your life partner or someone you work or spend time with on a regular basis, consider facing even a relatively small issue. Think of the grain of sand in the shoe. If you're in a sprint lasting only a few seconds, a grain of sand is no big deal. If, however, you are running a marathon, that grain of sand is going to end up hurting you a lot. (Trust me on this one.) Not only that, but the whole race is going to be about the grain of sand and nothing else.

In an important relationship, the smallest issue deserves to be faced and the fresh information it reveals folded into your mutual understandings and expectations.

⋄ *How important is the* **issue**? If the issue is, for instance, about my integrity, I will confront it with virtually anyone, regardless of the importance of our relationship. When one of your core values is called into question, or becomes an ingredient in a conflict, you are going to feel compelled to deal with it, even if it's with the person at the checkout stand at the grocery store, or a person you meet at a workshop, or someone you barely know. Ask yourself what will be the impact of this Pinch on your ability to accomplish the mission associated with this issue.

⋄ *What will happen in the* **future** *if I don't bring it up?* Can you live with it if the thing someone does that is a Pinch for you keeps happening indefinitely? What will be the future effect—on your relationship, the work that needs to get done, or on you personally or professionally—if you do nothing? If, in fact, it is something you can live with without resentment or any stuff going into your gunnysack, then let it slide, but the minute you become aware of even a little bit of resentment, bring it up—to keep it from moving into a Crunch.

⋄ *What will be the impact on your* **confidence** *and* **self-concept** *if you do not face it?* Many of us have had an early experience or two of failure in attempting to deal with a Pinch or a conflict. The tiger got *us*. We may have walked away from those experiences having learned that it is not a good thing to do, or, more significantly, that we are not able to successfully face a tiger. There is a great Zen saying: *If you can't, you must*. As a swimmer at Roanoke College, I recall standing on the diving board one afternoon as our Coach, Frances Ramser, challenged me to practice again a dive I had just messed up big time. "Do I have to?" I asked, hopefully. "No," she said. "You can step down off the board now if you want, or even do another, easier, dive; but if you want to be a diver, yep. You've got to try it again. If you don't, you'll never have that dive. That dive will always *have you*." Sometimes you need to face a tiger just because you need to re-discover that you can.

What Actually Confronts You?

Your tiger might not involve another person. It might be a tough decision you have been putting off, or a challenging meeting you need to lead, or some disruptive change that is happening, or even a question about your life direction. Anything that stands out from the normal flow of things, that has you concerned.

As you think about what confronts you, it is crucial that you 'clean up' your description of what is happening. I can almost guarantee that what you think is the tiger, is actually contaminated by your story about it and/or your judgments about it. Most people, when they start to describe the tiger, are coloring the experience, covering over what is happening in the real world with their stuff, judgments, labels, emotional freight. You cannot turn the experience into a lesson until you have separated out your baggage from the actual experience.

So, the first step in taking on Question 1: WHAT CONFRONTS ME? is to describe what is happening in the real world *without any spin or labeling*. If you had a video of what was going on that bugged you, what would a neutral observer actually *see* and *hear*? Not your interpretations, but the other person's behavior. This is hard to do, especially when you are upset, but it must be done. If you can't see what is happening, you will not be able to see what it means. You will not be able to get the lesson that is there for you. Instead, you are likely to end up being 'right' one more time, and reinforcing the story you already have about what they are doing and what it means.

How clean is this one:

"Oh, yeah, have I got a tiger to face! It's that jerk that shares my cubicle at work. What an idiot. He's always socializing and schmoozing with people, standing around and hovering over my shoulder, looking at what I am doing on my computer."

Is there any clean description here? I can't see it. Terms like jerk and idiot and even socializing, schmoozing, and hovering are all interpretive. Even if everyone you know would agree with you about those words, they are still *in you* and not actually *in* the other person. What does he *say* or *do* that leads you to label him with terms like idiot or jerk? I might give you "looking at what I am doing on my computer," but even that requires some interpretation.

Let's see what can be said with all the interpretive stuff peeled away:

"Occasionally during the day, two or three people come and stand beside my cubicle mate's chair, talking with each other and with him, at times when I am busy and want more privacy."

The Practice: *Name The Trigger Moment*

Take a piece of paper—or your computer—and write down what the other person does that bugs you. Then read it over slowly and carefully, looking for any words that are not pure description. You want to end up with words that would cleanly describe what anyone would see or hear on a video of the situation. You might even ask a good friend to read it over with you, helping you look for your interpretive stuff that you might think is clean.

Once you have this moment or experience written down cleanly, you are ready to take on Question 2: What Am I Bringing?

Question 2: What am I bringing?

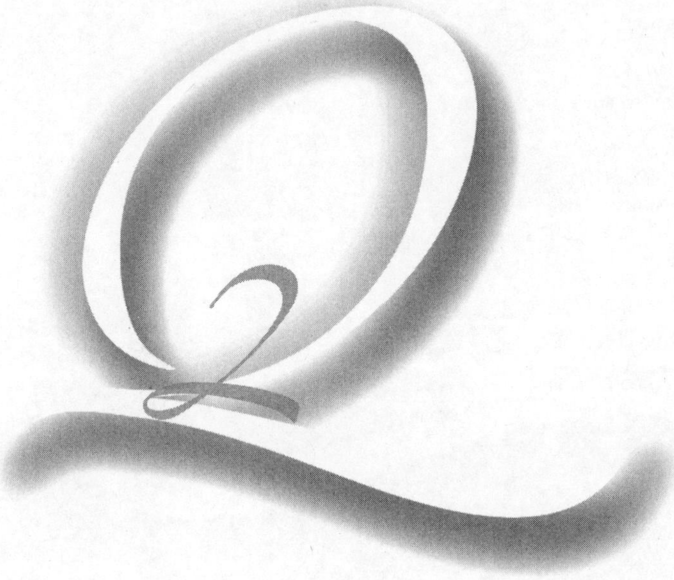

Chapter Four

The Space Where Everything Happens

As you turn toward that tiger that confronts you at work, or elsewhere, what are you *bringing* to the situation? These would be your expectations, your assumptions, your history with this person, your hopes and fears. In short, *what do you want to happen as a result of exploring what is going on?*

Take great care here. Your response to this second of the FIVE QUESTIONS will determine how much value you get out of this process. *What am I bringing?* is a powerful question, possibly *the* most powerful question you could ever ask yourself, because your answer creates the space for everything that happens next. It determines what you are able to *see* and *experience*. You are going to find what you are looking for. If you happen to discover something else, something different—possibly more valuable, it will be pure chance, or a result of your expanding awareness or your changing what you are seeking. I call it grace.

How powerful is what you bring to a 'moment?' Here's an immediate example: Why did you pick up this book?

Let's say you are looking for a few personal development tips and techniques. Then that's what you will find here. If, on the other hand, you are looking for a transformational process, something that strengthens the very foundation of your life, then that's what you will find here.

Where you are coming from determines where you end up. Someone I have come to respect a great deal, General Rick Hillier, Chief of Canadian Forces, says to his people, "When you get a chance, *go big*." Why not? Bring the biggest, most important questions or issues you are aware of right now to this book, enlarge what you expect to the most incredible outcome you can imagine, and let the material have its way with you.

The Carpet Expert And The Electrician

What you bring not only determines what you will get out of reading this book, it also determines what you see and experience in every interaction you have. It couldn't be any other way. As I alluded to before, there is a wonderful ancient Sufi saying that says, *"When a pickpocket walks up to a spiritual teacher, all he sees are pockets."* The potential for the pickpocket in an encounter with a profound transformational presence is huge, but if all he/she sees is another 'mark,' it reduces the value of the exchange to how much money the teacher is carrying, or how smooth will be the 'lift.' What a shame. A missed opportunity.

Here's another example. If a carpet expert walked into the room where you are, what would she notice without even having to think about it? What could she tell you with little or no conscious effort? In a matter of a few seconds, she could probably tell you (with amazing accuracy) the square footage of the room, the thread count of the carpet, its cost, its durability, and whether the colors 'work' or not. She notices the carpet because of what she 'brings' to the experience.

If an electrician walked in right behind her—again without any conscious thinking—what would he notice? Probably how many outlets there are on the walls, where they are placed, the sufficiency and location of the lighting system, etc. What would he likely *not* notice? Among other things, he might miss the carpet entirely! As a result of what he 'brings,' the electrician will see things that are important to him and miss other important things, as will the carpet expert. Each brings a different set of eyes, expectations, and sense of what is important to the room, and what they bring virtually determines the shape and size of what is available to them.

The Human Brain

Researchers have determined that the human brain is processing four hundred billion bits of information each second. That could be overwhelming, but our minds are aware of only two thousand of those bits. Our internal system is filtering out 99.99999% of what is coming in, and attending to the little that is left. There is even research that documents what the eye 'sees' in TV ads. Using a scanner that can determine where a viewer's eyes are focusing, marketers can find out what kind of images are more likely to be looked at or, I would say, seen. What those watching are seeing is being shaped by what they each bring to the scenes being shown. As you might expect, men and women 'see' different facets of what is shown, as do older versus younger viewers, as do people from different cultures. Even within those larger samples, individuals notice different nuances as well.

We human beings are walking around all day looking out at what is happening and yet only attending to an infinitely small percentage of what is there for us to see. It's scary to think about what we are *missing* as a result of the filters we bring to each encounter with the world. Imagine how, like the pickpocket standing beside a spiritual teacher and seeing only pockets, we are limiting the possibilities by reducing our world to what we have come to know and expect.

The Impossible Possibility

It is possible to shift what you are bringing, however. In the seminar based on the FIVE QUESTIONS, some people are 'sent' by their boss or life partner. This means they show up on the first day grudgingly pursuing someone else's agenda for them. We tell them that if they are sitting there for someone else's reasons, they are not in the room yet. We suggest that the program will actually start for them the instant they come up with a reason of their own for being there.

Some people come looking for leadership or

interpersonal techniques they can use on others. Another missed opportunity. What a tiny thing to be after. That is why in the Pre-Work we ask participants to do before they arrive, and on the first day, we challenge them to take on Question 2: WHAT AM I BRINGING? The invitation is to expand what they came for, to go for something really huge, something they may even have considered out of reach. We challenge them to go for what I call an impossible possibility.

An impossible possibility is something that you know is theoretically possible but, from where you are standing, appears to be highly unlikely or completely out of reach. See how a shift in what a few recent seminar participants 'brought' opened the door to greater possibilities:

> ⋄   The initial question: *How can I get my spouse to stop hounding me about not being home enough? I feel guilty enough as it is.*

> ⋄   The impossible possibility: *How can I double my results at work while also doubling the time I spend with my family?*

> ⋄   The initial question: *How can I get that person at work to stop causing me and my colleagues so much trouble?*

> ⋄   The impossible possibility: *How can I gain access to a way of working with conflict so everyone wins and no one is damaged?*

> ◇ The initial question: *Why can't we make more profit from our seminars?*

> ◇ The impossible possibility: *How can we effortlessly fill our programs with people who gladly pay top dollar for the privilege?*

What if you approached your interactions with other people, especially the challenging ones, as potentially transformational experiences, expanding and deepening who you are—thus maximizing your contribution to life. It's not that complicated. It simply requires you to become aware of what you are bringing, and to ask whether that is large enough. To open yourself to expanding and deepening possibility in your life, start asking yourself questions like these:

◇ Is where I am coming from in this interaction worthy of who we are?

◇ What am I 'bringing' to this moment—and how is that affecting what could happen?

◇ What am I missing in this situation that could change the way it turns out?

◇ What is an impossible possibility worth going for here?

Asking questions like these will begin to crack open the door into those rooms in the mansion of your soul that haven't seen much light. Exploring every one of those rooms and embracing what you find there is what life is all about. In words attributed to Jesus, one of our best-known teachers: "*I have come that you might have life, and have it more abundantly.*" To further clarify his meaning, the root meaning of the Aramaic word behind 'abundant' means something like 'pushed out in all directions, complete, no place left unknown, unexplored or unexpressed.'

How abundant is your life? Does something in you need to expand or deepen or let go or shift? If so, the FIVE QUESTIONS will be of great value to you but not in the way you may be thinking. It's not about changing anything. *Remember, you don't need to change yourself; you need to become yourself—and that changes everything.*

The Objective: Purpose, Power, And Peace

"Okay," you say, "I'm game—how do I 'become myself?' That sounds almost trite. I am what I am, as Popeye says. How can I be anything other than who I am?" Or, as one manager/engineer said recently at a seminar, "*Becoming myself?! What a bunch of California hot tub bullshit. Let's just dance around a candle and sing Kum Baya. ...*" That was on Day 1. You should have seen him on Day 4, emotionally talking excitedly about his new self-awareness and commitment to go back to his home and work, bringing all he now knew he could be. "*I can't wait to unleash myself back there!*"

As you will soon see, the chances are slim that you are currently walking around being 'abundant'—fully who you are, pushed out in all directions, complete. Instead, as you will see in Question 3: WHAT RUNS ME?, you are likely operating in a kind of autopilot mode, going through your days trying to be somebody you believe or hope the world around you will 'buy.' While that is going on, who you *are,* that golden center or central core of your being—that place from which all your gifts and talents emanate—is yearning to find expression in your work and life.

In an abundant life, *all* of who you are is freely and powerfully expressed into the world, without apology, in a way that makes a difference—to you, to those around you, and to life itself. The gap between who you truly are on the inside and how much of that you allow to manifest on the outside is an inverse measure of your experience of purpose, power, and peace. The smaller the gap, the more purpose, power, and peace you will know.

◇   PURPOSE—This means having a deep sense of mission or direction in your life where a large chunk of who you *are* is focused in the service of something greater than yourself. Taking on the FIVE QUESTIONS can lead you to discover—or re-discover— what we call a Greater Purpose, a path for yourself that nurtures your own soul or spirit, contributes greatly to those around you and is in alignment with what is being called for by life (the larger context in which you find yourself).

◇   POWER—Do you wish you had more control or even influence over what happens to you?

Adapting what poet David White says, "The ego's goal is to have power *over* what happens to you. The soul's goal is to have power *through* what happens to you—whatever that might be." Your default approach to life and work may give the illusion or hope of control, but there are only three things over which you have direct control: what you *say*, what you *do* and—the most important—what you *intend*. Taking on the FIVE QUESTIONS can show you how to manage those to give you *real* power, and the capacity to live and work with greater confidence.

⋄ PEACE—The sense of greater purpose and authentic power *through* life also brings with it a definite calmness or peace. People who are applying the FIVE QUESTIONS report a sense of rightness with things, even situations that before were full of conflict and pain. When you learn how to engage the world from that inner place where dwells the highest and best of who you are, grace and peace are the natural result.

Let's take another important area—leadership. The gap between who you *are* and what you *present* to the world is also a predictor of your *effectiveness*, whether you are a leader, a manager, a parent, a life partner, or simply a member of an organization or community. Closing that gap can make you a compassionate force to be reckoned with—the goal of any true leader.

Summary

Think about your 'tiger' situation. What are you 'bringing' in terms of:

- ❖ your *history* with the people involved?

- ❖ your expectations—for yourself, for them, for the situation?

- ❖ your assumptions?

- ❖ your fears or concerns?

- ❖ your wants, needs, and/or requirements?

- ❖ your commitments—to yourself, to them, to the situation?

Getting clear about what you bring prepares you to take a long, hard look at what will be running you as you face the tiger. How are you 'on automatic' without realizing it? How does that affect everything you do? You may be surprised at what you will discover about yourself as you take on the next question: WHAT RUNS ME?

Question 3: What runs me?

Chapter Five

Living on Automatic

You may think you are in charge of your life and your decisions. Wrong—unless you have done some long and deep work on yourself. What if I told you that your life is being run by something—or someone—*inside you* that is basing decisions on what may have been true a long time ago, but is now no longer necessary—and no longer serving you?

You live a lot of your life on automatic and don't realize it.

A few common examples:

◇   The next time you get dressed, notice how you put on your shoes and socks, how you brush your hair, how you put on your pants or slacks. The other day I did, and was struck by how *automatic* it was. Even the choice of which clothes to buy and wear are made within a relatively narrow band of what is appropriate or attractive or weird or 'what's me/not me.' There are millions of clothing options out there that you never even consider, unconsciously staying inside what is familiar or 'right' for you.

⬦ How many times have you gotten in your car, driven somewhere and, on arriving, realized that you can't remember much at all about the trip? During the drive you were making lots of decisions—turn here, shift gears here, put your signal on here, go slower here; but they weren't actually conscious decisions, where you thought about what you were going to do and then acted. The actions you took were a result of habitual patterns that have by now taken on an automatic quality.

⬦ When was the last time you were interacting with someone you have difficulty getting along with and they said something that set you off? If you look at your response, you may realize how predictable it was—how automatic. When someone says or does X, you have virtually the same reaction every time: You think, feel, and do some variation of Y.

So, while you may think you're walking around freely making decisions all day long, you don't realize how much of what you say and do every day is 'more of the same.' There may be some variation, but it is almost always variation within limits, like going faster or slower in first gear. You know how it is with a loved one or work partner: One of you says something and off you go into a predictable pattern of interactions that can go all night, all weekend—or for the rest of your lives together! You may think you're doing things differently, but it is change within the same paradigm.

What makes this so important is that most of us:

- ✧ don't realize that we are, in fact, operating inside an old, out-of-date paradigm,
- ✧ can't see how that limits our options and, therefore,
- ✧ rarely experience truly fresh moments, and
- ✧ are unable to create transformation in our lives.

Here's how it works:

The Human Autopilot: Your Personal Default Operating System

When you wake up in the morning and 'boot up' (turn on your conscious mind), what comes on-line first—to continue the computer analogy—is your own personal operating system. I call it the autopilot because it is essentially the automatic, habitual, unconscious, default way you navigate your way through life. In aviation, planes are equipped with a guidance system, called the automatic pilot, which is capable of steering the craft to a pre-set destination without any action required from the pilot. Even if the pilot goes to sleep, or becomes unconscious for some reason, the autopilot takes the plane where it has been programmed to go.

At the human level, as you will see, your autopilot influences the kinds of jobs you take on, the kinds of people you are drawn to—or not drawn to—the kinds of clothes you wear, the body you develop, and all the thoughts and judgments you have about yourself, others, and life. It is nearly impossible to think *about* your autopilot because you think *from* it. This is because your autopilot is not *made up* of thoughts; it *generates* your thoughts.

What Happened To Free Will?

At this point, you may have an internal argument taking place. "I am *not* on automatic! I am not a robot. I have free will. I do what I want. I make my own choices about all those things. *Nobody* tells *me* how to dress or what job to take."

Would that it were so. It is true that our minds make what appear to be freely chosen decisions all the time. What we fail to understand is that the range of options we have available to us from which we choose is severely limited in ways we do not understand.

We all walk around inside a learned view of reality—our 'default World' in the diagram on the next page.

Your 'default world' includes your deep programming, your core beliefs about yourself, other people, and about life. These are not *thoughts,* they are rather the fundamental elements in your operating system, from which most of your thoughts originate.

What you notice is what you then *see* as you look out at things, based on this world view. You see what you see. Two people can be present for the same event (a movie, a conversation, a meeting, a book) and yet report two very different experiences of what happened. As you will see in Question 5: WHAT WILL UNLEASH ME?, this is not only possible, but inevitable.

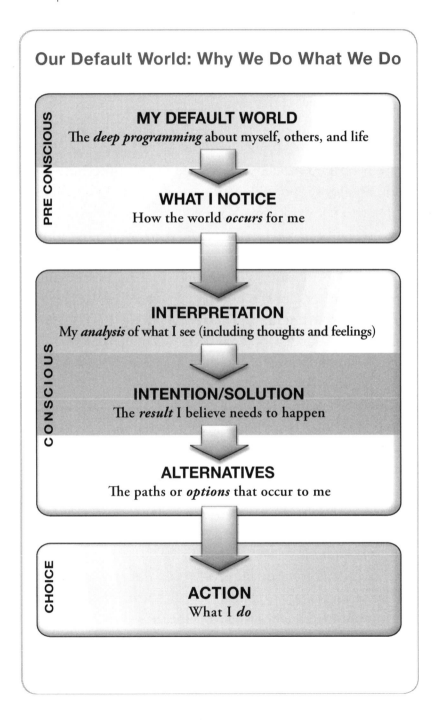

Our Default World: Why We Do What We Do

PRE CONSCIOUS

MY DEFAULT WORLD
The *deep programming* about myself, others, and life

WHAT I NOTICE
How the world *occurs* for me

CONSCIOUS

INTERPRETATION
My *analysis* of what I see (including thoughts and feelings)

INTENTION/SOLUTION
The *result* I believe needs to happen

ALTERNATIVES
The paths or *options* that occur to me

CHOICE

ACTION
What I *do*

Your past history has ground the lenses through which you see what is happening around—and inside—you. You literally cannot see something that is not already in your 'library' of that-which-is.

The Wristwatch On The Ground

It may be hard to accept that we can't see something we don't believe is possible, but have a look at an example I heard at a workshop I attended. Marilyn Ferguson, author of *The Aquarian Conspiracy*, related this fascinating story from the last century.

A group of cultural anthropologists was studying perception among the aboriginal people of Australia. In one experiment, they drew a circle in the dirt and placed several objects inside: a pencil, a shoe, a watch, and some aboriginal tools. As members of the group came up one by one, they were asked to pick up everything inside the circle. After a few people had done this, the researchers noticed that each person had picked up everything, *except the wristwatch*. After each stopped, the scientists began to ask, "Have you picked up everything you see inside the circle on the ground?" Each Aborigine would indicate yes and yet, there on the ground at their feet, inside the circle, lay the wristwatch.

What was going on here, the researchers wondered? Why aren't they picking up the watch? Using a principle from science called Occam's Razor—where you take the simplest hypothesis that explains the most variables—they determined that the reason people had not picked up the watch was because *they couldn't see it.* You might ask, "What do you mean, they couldn't see it? The doggone thing was right there on the ground!" Yes, but without any experiential referent for 'wristwatch,' they were unable to see it. To them it probably looked like an interesting patch of ground. They had no category in their experiential library for wristwatch. They could differentiate the pencil (they had stick in their world-view) and the hammer (tool), but not wristwatch. They were unable to distinguish it from everything else. You and I will not be able to see or hear something in front of us for which we do not have a referent in our conceptual map of reality. Here's another example that may be a little closer to home.

Kurt: A Hard Man To Work For

Just in case you don't buy that story from the outback, here's another, taken from a Washington, D.C. organizational setting. As part of an executive team development session for a client a few years ago, I spoke with the CEO about my findings from data-gathering interviews conducted with his vice presidents. Among the feedback items was the comment from several of them that the boss was "a hard man to work for." They said he rarely gave people positive feedback, frequently finding something to criticize. This led his team members to avoid him, some with gut-wrenching fear dominating their days at work.

When I told him, he was stunned. "That can't be! They're the best people around," he said, "and if that changes, I'll fire them!" He caught what he had said, gave a rueful chuckle and said, "Okay, I got it.

I've got really high standards for them. Sounds like I'm creating a problem for them—and for myself—that we don't need. What should I do about it?" I suggested that at the team development offsite retreat the next day he should look for opportunities to "catch someone doing something right," as management expert Ken Blanchard suggests.* "When you do," I went on, "tell them right away—authentically—what you saw them do that you appreciate." He acknowledged that was going to be a challenge but, with some encouragement, he said he'd give it a shot.

The next day, as we worked our way down the agenda, I noticed that Sue, the marketing VP, was starting to act nervous. "What's going on?" I asked her quietly at a break.

"Well, when the VPs met yesterday to decide who would bring up each agenda item, no one wanted to do the 'Feedback to Kurt' piece, so we drew straws. I lost. I'm expecting to get fired." I encouraged her, and said Kurt had been coached to be more open, and that she should expect something different from him. Disbelieving, she went back in the room, and later in the afternoon, it was time for her report.

"Kurt, I have to tell you that I drew the short straw on this one!" Nervous laughter rippled around the room as the two people on either side of her tried surreptitiously to slide their chairs farther away from Sue. The danger they were anticipating: 'Organizational Lightning,' as some readers will recognize.

"I have learned more from you about this field in the five years I have worked for you than I could even imagine,"

* Blanchard, Kenneth and Spencer Johnson, *The One Minute Manager*, William Morrow, New York 1982

Sue went on, "but I have to tell you that for the past year or so, I have felt like quitting."

"Why is that?" Kurt asked, genuinely curious.

"Well, for one thing, you never tell me if I've done a good job. Instead, you stick your head in the cubby and say things like, 'There's a typo on Page 25!' or 'Those figures on Page 38 don't add up to 100%,' or 'Where's that report I asked you for last Friday?' I know what you *don't* like about my work. What I can't take is not knowing what, if anything, you *value* about me or my work."

The whole room held its breath as Kurt gathered himself to respond. I muttered a short prayer, something along the lines of, "Please, Kurt, do the right thing here!"

"Sue, first of all, thanks for telling me this. I don't like hearing it, but I think you are onto something about me. I have had a problem ever since I was a kid giving compliments to people. I think it's because I don't want them to see me as phony. But you know what? It took a lot of courage for you to stand up and say that to me, and I want you to know how much I appreciate you for that." You could have heard a pin drop in that room.

Then Sue blurted, "And another thing is ..."

The room erupted. Stunned, Sue said, "What?! What is everyone so excited about?"

"Sue!" one of the other VPs shouted, "Kurt just did what you said he never does. He gave you a compliment. He said he appreciated your courage in standing up and telling him all that!"

"No, he didn't," she said. *"He would never say that!"*

She flat missed it. When Kurt did something that

did not exist as a possibility in Sue's world—like the wristwatch on the ground for the Aborigines—she couldn't see it. She *knew* who Kurt was. He was someone who never gave positive feedback. Given that core belief, she *had* to miss it. Otherwise, if by some miracle she had 'seen' it, she would have had to revise her entire world view and, even more difficult, let go of the deep programming on which those unconscious beliefs rested. "He would never say that!" She could have passed a lie detector test on what she believed she had heard, that's how deep was her certainty about who Kurt 'was,' what he did—and did not do.

It took almost an hour and several colleagues working with Sue for her to even open to the possibility that Kurt had in fact expressed appreciation to her—and meant it. I'm not sure to this day that she truly believes he said it.

We See What We 'Know'

So, back to the diagram: We are only able to see those things that already exist in the pantry of our mind, which come from our unique experiences, our unique history. More accurately, we see things in terms of our worldview. It's kind of scary to realize that as we look out at the world we are actually seeing our own history in front of us. But how could it be any other way? How could we see something that doesn't exist in our map or reality?

Consider a union-management meeting where one party comes out with a genuinely conciliatory offer. How is the other side likely to hear it? "It's a ploy, a trick. Where's the catch?" The world 'shows up' for us in terms of images present in our deep programming. All this is pre-conscious, automatic, out of our direct control.

What we notice leads us to an Interpretation, an analysis of what is going on, our thoughts and feelings *about* what we see. At this point, our perception becomes conscious and we are aware that we are seeing something. Our Interpretation is accompanied by an Intention, something we want or think we need out of the situation, a result or solution that we believe would be a good thing. That leads us to start considering Alternatives, a range of options we might choose to do. Sooner or later, we choose one and end up taking action.

Can you see that each step in this virtually instantaneous process serves to narrow down the possibilities present in the next step? By the time we get to considering alternatives, there are literally millions of options that never even occur to us, given the trip we just made down what I call the diagnostic funnel.

This complex process is going on every second we are awake. It happens in nanoseconds. The key to it all is our Autopilot, our ancient, bone-deep programming, which drives everything we see, feel, think, and do. Where, then, did that all-powerful worldview come from?

Chapter Six

Somebody Training

If you are alive, you are equipped with an Autopilot, and it was programmed very early on with instructions on where to go and how to get there. Actually, instead of saying that you have an Autopilot, it would be more accurate to say that your Autopilot *has you.*

As former Harvard Professor and spiritual development coach Ram Dass liked to put it, the moment you emerged from the womb, you were enrolled in Somebody Training. As a little one lying in the crib, unbeknownst to you, you were in a virtual classroom, being taught by the other somebodies around you to 'be somebody.' More than likely your Faculty didn't realize what they were doing. They were just loving you the best they could—which might have been a lot—and trying to raise you right. Everything they said and did around you became part of your Somebody Training Curriculum. Even in situations where the classroom wasn't so loving, and where your Faculty was a negative example, you were still in a Somebody Training course.

It is important to note that the program you were enrolled in was not training you to be just *any* Somebody. You were learning to be a *particular kind of Somebody*—the kind of Somebody that your Faculty believed would have a chance to make it in the world. Just as parents in every species of animals on the planet do what they can to prepare their offspring to survive, your parents and other adjunct faculty did what they could to equip you for life as they believed it to be.

Hard Evidence Of My Somebody Training

Not long ago, out of the blue, I received a package of old letters and photos in the mail, sent from my cousin, Elizabeth, who had discovered them while going through her mother's things after her death. As I read the letters, written to me and to my grandfather by my own mother when I was a child, I was stunned and then moved to tears by what I heard in them. It dawned on me that I was actually *looking at* the outline of the Curriculum from my Somebody Training, embedded in the letters!

First, some background. When they were written, I was almost two years old. My father—already a full-blown alcoholic—had taken a job as a newspaperman with *The Washington Post* in Washington, DC, and my mother had gone with him, working as a secretary for the Navy Department. I was left in Richmond, Virginia, three hours away, to live with my grandfather (a Lutheran minister), my grandmother, various aunts and uncles, Annabelle (a maid), and Sister Ruth (a Lutheran Deaconess). All these people loved me dearly. As the Scherer namesake—I am John Jacob Scherer IV—and the apple of their eye, I received a lot of attention and affection from them all. In retrospect, the painful fact was that Mom and Pop were not there for me, and only came down from DC to visit me every two or three weeks, leaving a crying little boy to find his way with everyone else.

Listen to these two unedited letters from my mother (one to me and one to my grandfather) and see if you can discern aspects of the curriculum that became a central part of little Johnny Scherer's Somebody Training.

1322 L Street NW
Washington, D.C.
April 6, 1942

Dear Son:

    It was too bad that I had to leave when you were so upset and mad at your mother. I had hoped that you would be asleep by the time my bus left, but you seemed to sense the fact that I was going to leave last night and couldn't go to sleep. If you think you missed me this morning, you really ought to have seen your mother looking around for her little man when she first woke up and then remembering that it would be about two weeks

before she could see him again! 'Fa-voo'
asked me about you and I was so upset that I
told him about our last little contretemps.

Sometimes when I think it over, it seems
best that I don't come down there and get you
all upset, because the emotional excitement
is not good for you. It is entirely selfishness
that prompts me to visit you, little man. You
would be a lot better off if I didn't do it. But
I do hope you can bear up under it and not let
it worry you too much. Try not to give them
too much trouble over it.

Please thank the folks for such a nice
Easter and for taking such grand care of
you for me. Pretty soon now I should be able
to repay them in some measure. Tomorrow I'm
going to buy you some little suits for the
warm weather and a shift or two. You are
popping out of everything else.

Give our love to all the folks, and
tell Grandpa to save a day sometime for that
fishing trip. Pop and I would both like to
go the first chance we get. Be good and take
care of things.

Bons baisers,

Mother

(Fluent in French, Mom often closed her letters to me
with that phrase, which means 'good kisses.')

Somebody Training Curriculum

What embedded messages do *you* see? Here are the embedded messages from my Somebody Training that I have been able to recognize in this letter, expanded and generalized based on what I read in them today.

```
Dear Son:

        It was too bad that I had to leave when
you were so upset and mad at your mother.
I had hoped that you would be asleep by the
time my bus left, but you seemed to sense the
fact that I was going to leave last night and
couldn't go to sleep.
```

Embedded Somebody Training Message: *Don't get upset or angry—even about something as painful as your mother leaving and not coming back for two weeks. Getting upset is bad.*

```
        If you think you missed me this
morning, you really ought to have seen your
mother looking around for her little man when
she first woke up and then remembering that
it would be about two weeks before she could
see him again! 'Fa-voo' asked me about you
and I was so upset that I told him about our
last little contretemps.
```

Embedded Message: *It's your fault that your mom misses you, as is the fact that when you get upset you cause 'contretemps' (arguments or conflicts).*

```
        Sometimes when I think it over, it seems
best that I don't come down there and get you
all upset, because the emotional excitement
is not good for you.
```

Embedded Message: *Emotional excitement is a bad thing, and something to be avoided. Wanting something (having my mom there with me) will result in people being less inclined to do the thing you yearn for. Don't yearn for anything; you won't get it anyway.*

It is entirely selfishness that prompts me to visit you, little man. You would be a lot better off if I didn't do it. But I do hope you can bear up under it and not let it worry you too much. Try not to give them too much trouble over it.

Embedded Message: *I love you, but what you feel (e.g. the worry in your heart) is not good for you—or for those around you. You can't trust your feelings. Don't let your feelings be a problem for those around you. Keep your emotions under control at all times.*

Please thank the folks for such a nice Easter and for taking such grand care of you for me. Pretty soon now I should be able to repay them in some measure. Tomorrow I'm going to buy you some little suits for the warm weather and a shift or two. You are popping out of everything else.

Embedded Message: *Your being where you are creates a debt which I will have to try to repay someday—but probably won't be able to. Your presence is a burden.*

Give our love to all the folks, and tell Grandpa to save a day sometime for that fishing trip. Pop and I would both like to go the first chance we get. Be good and take care of things.

Embedded Somebody Training Message: *You are responsible for 'taking care of things'—even when you are only 18 months old.*

See how this early Autopilot programming works? Those messages from my mother came from an innocent and loving intent. She had no desire to embed teachings in her letters that would create life challenges for her only child years down the road, but she did—and they did.

Here is another example, a letter my mother sent two days later to my grandfather, whose nickname was 'Judge' to his close friends and family. Even though this letter—and others like it, I'm sure—never got read to me, they were reflective of the 'energy field' inside which I was being raised. It reveals the psychological 'music' playing in the family circle that my Faculty resonated with.

1322 L Street, N.W.
Washington, D.C.
April 8, 1942

Dear Judge:

How is my little man behaving himself these days? I do hope he was not too much trouble to handle yesterday and that someone is going to try to curb that temper of his.

Somebody Training Message: *Don't let Johnny be trouble for people. Make sure he is easy to get along with. Don't allow him to have and express 'negative' feelings.*

It was most reassuring to me to see you use a firm voice and expression with him the other night. Really, Judge, it will be a kindness to him in the long run to let him understand that the world was not made for him and that people are not just hanging on his every word and ready to give him everything he wants, or thinks he wants.

Somebody Training Message: *The world is not going to respond to John's needs. What he wants is not important—and is not going to happen, so help him learn not to want anything and/or to make do with whatever he has.*

He must not get a distorted view of the world and people. It might ruin him permanently to find out some time later that we were all wrong, that there are other people, that he must share things, that he must work for things and that things do not always work out as we think they should. You ought to be able to tell him that God has plans for us other than the ones we figure out.

Somebody Training Messages: *John's natural view of the way things are is not valid. For instance, he must earn everything that comes to him. Help him see that there is no free lunch.*

Give our love to all the folks. Take care of yourself, Judge. Kiss my boy.

Boone

Aren't these letters amazing things to have? (Thank you, Elizabeth.) They are a literary and literal Time Capsule. It's as if I am able to listen in on my mother's heart 60+ years ago as she tried to be the very best mom she could be, given the circumstances—and her own Somebody Training. I want the reader to understand clearly that I loved my mom a great deal and, since her death at our home in 1991, love her even more, as I have discovered and explored the world of *her* Somebody Training. From this perspective, I now see how her love and concern for me got translated into these 'lessons,' which ironically and inevitably coupled a positive *intention* with a negative *impact*.

Your parents and other family members did something like this with you. In intending to shape you into a Somebody who could make it in the world, the impact of their training became both a blessing and a curse, an asset and a liability. In their classroom you learned about yourself, other people, and life. The lessons went deep, living invisibly in your 'bones.' So here you are, years later, still being run by this early programming, now encoded into your Autopilot.

The Upside Of My Somebody Training

My Somebody Training (just like yours) was not all bad. It contained not only things I needed to build *over*, but also things I could build *on*. As a child growing up in the Scherer Somebody Training Program, I learned to be a 'good boy,' to put others' needs before my own, hoping that my Faculty would be proud of me—and love me. I remember clearly my grandmother telling me,

"Johnny, God comes first, other people come second, and you come third, w-a-y down the line."

I became an Eagle Scout, was awarded the Chamber of Commerce Junior Citizen Award in the Eighth Grade, and did everything I could—and made sure I *didn't* do other things—to protect the good name of the Scherer family. I set about mastering 'the manly arts' required in Virginia at that time: athletics (swimming, running, tennis, all the ball sports), self-defense (boxing and wrestling), being a gentleman (things like opening doors and standing for women, waiting for the hostess to lift her fork before eating, not taking the last serving of anything, etc.).

Blend the five generations of Lutheran ministers in the gene pool on my father's side, and Daniel Boone's brother William on my mother's side, and you've got quite a Faculty heritage! It has taken many years of hard inner work, however—a lot of it using the FIVE QUESTIONS—to find my way through those old messages to a more authentic, soulful, and unleashed way of being.

The fundamental upside of my early Somebody Training is a bone-deep tendency to approach life as *a pioneer with spirit, capable of working on the fringes of the ordinary, committed to creating a better world.* I am sure my Faculty would be proud of me. In retrospect, I am still following the early guidance of my Somebody Training program, and often the results are positive. I can see the footprints of that training in each of the several kinds of work I have done in my life. In the Navy as Combat Officer on board a destroyer, I saw my real work as helping the people around me do a better job and yet grow personally at the same time. Then more directly, as Lutheran Chaplain at Cornell University, my work was one hundred percent about serving the world. Later, when two colleagues and I started the country's first truly competency-based graduate program in applied behavioral science, my work as core faculty involved teaching mid-career professionals how to create positive change, starting with themselves. Some years later, I began my consulting and speaking career, and FIVE QUESTIONS is one of the outcomes.

Recently the Stephen Covey organization selected me as one of America's top 100 Thought Leaders in Personal/Leadership Development. Sharing the list with people like Wayne Dyer, Oprah, Lance Armstrong, and Mark Victor Hanson made me think that Mom and Pop and my other Somebody Training Faculty would have been relieved that all the 'stuff' happening in my early years apparently had not ruined me.

One element programmed into my Autopilot— the desire to serve others and be a positive force in virtually every situation where I find myself—has led, I believe, to many lives and organizations being transformed. I wonder from time to time how many people are walking around today who, from time to time, are remembering and possibly appreciating the role my work played in helping them shape the lives they are living. As you will see in exploring Question 4: WHAT CALLS ME?, unleashing the human spirit is not something I *do*, it's simply who I *am*.

The mischief inherent in your Somebody Training is not that when you 'graduate' you are doing bad things, it's in *having to do* what you find yourself doing—automatically. When you break the automatic quality of what you do, it may look to an outsider like you are doing many of the exact same things, but they will be more authentic and, as you will see, less manipulative.

The Downside Of My Somebody Training

⬦ MAKING REQUESTS. As a deck officer aboard our US Navy destroyer, I had no trouble giving orders with clarity and authority: *"Right full rudder! All ahead Two Thirds!"* However, getting people to do what I want them to do has sometimes been surprisingly hard over the years, even a request as simple as: "Colleen, I need you to get this report out to the client by 4:00pm today. I don't care what it takes!" Even more challenging: "Could I have a hug?" I am now able to ask for what I want, but the old internal 'tape' still whispers when I do, "Johnny, you're going to be disappointed. Remember, if you are too forceful you could make life hard for someone else—and that's a big No-No."

⬦ EMOTIONS. If you were to ask me how I felt about something, I would probably say, "Let me think about that for a minute." I am almost always able to locate what I am feeling and report it out—or express it, but I seem to be using my *mind* as a search engine and a handle for dealing with the emotion that reveals itself. This works, but I envy the people who experience their feelings more directly.

◇ INTIMACY. I thought I would be married to the same person for fifty years, have 2.4 children, a Ford station wagon, and a brick home in Virginia. That is how the script was begun, but not how it turned out. I have been married three times, each time to an amazing and wonderful woman. When my older son got married a few years ago, all three of my ex-wives were there, clustered in conversation like sorority sisters. Each of them would probably tell you that I was hard to love, partly because of my tendency to 'leave,' to not be present when I was actually there, and also because of how challenging it was for me to confront strong negative emotions or conversations. It is not too much of an exaggeration to say that I still freeze like a deer in the headlights at the first sign that someone I care about is upset at me. I can move off that stuck place fairly quickly now, using 'unleashing' techniques from Question 5. That initial impulse to freeze is still there, automatic and unbidden, but now it triggers the new skill of recognizing and recovering.

So, Why Do You Do What You Do?

The short and simple answer is: your Somebody Training. Somebody Training is not a good thing. It's not a bad thing, either. It's a *human* thing. It's just the way it is. You are born—you start your Somebody

Training. You go along, trying your best to become the person you are supposed to be, until something in life forces or invites you to consider who *else* you might be. When you face a situation, a relationship, a challenge that just won't be handled by your operating the way you usually operate—using your Autopilot—you may feel like the Navy fighter pilots with whom I worked, who spoke occasionally of finding themselves "out of airspeed, altitude, and ideas."

When that happens, when life puts you in a situation where what usually works doesn't work anymore, the instinct is to simply turn up the volume on what you know best (your Autopilot) and try even harder to be your special Somebody. If and when *that* fails, you can find yourself in a truly pregnant moment, when you are radically ready to explore alternatives.

John Morrow: *The Wake-Up Call*
Often, this invitation takes the form of a wake-up call. I think of John Morrow, a bright, alive, on-purpose manager in the New York headquarters of a national association. "I was *sent* to this program," he said matter-of-factly at the opening session of his Intensive. "There's no delicate way to put it. Before I came, people had been telling me things like, 'You're really good, but ...' and 'John, you make your numbers and get results, but ...' I figured, with a no-kidding nudge from my boss, that it was time to find out about the 'but!' What I discovered was that while I was getting results I was also 'leaving a trail

of bodies,' or as one colleague put it, 'John, you're impressive, but you're an asshole.'

"At home, I was one kind of person: warm, understanding, able to take the long view, firm without being nasty. At work, though, I turned into some kind of monster: short with people—mean, actually—and wanting everything *now*, or else dire consequences would follow. It was almost a Jekyll and Hyde thing.

"What a delight to discover at my Intensive *another me* inside, one with interests and skills and qualities that I never knew I had, and then to discover, standing just behind him, in an inner 'center' (as I guess John Scherer would call it) my 'essence' or 'spirit,' which is able to bring the best attributes of both my inner worlds into play in appropriate ways. From this place, I have access to a perspective on things and people that is higher and broader than my previous normal operating mode. I learned to recognize what other people bring—not just what I *want* them to bring. I can now acknowledge the baggage that other people carry and how it impacts them (good or bad) and I accept working with that person—exactly the way he or she is, rather than as I think he or she should be.

"I saw that in the past my beating up on people was because they were not—in my mind at least—living up to the standards that I set for *myself*. 'If only they were as hard-working and dedicated as I was, they would see my point and we would get the job done!' Because they were not being the image that I set for ME, I beat them up! Isn't that ironic? Now I can see more clearly and accurately what is happening, inside myself and with other people. I can also bring the way I am at home to work. What a difference it has made."

Eight months later, John, the guy who wasn't sure whether he would keep his job, was selected Vice President of his organization, something that just wasn't in the cards prior to his doing his inner work of self-discovery and recognition. Apart from this rather significant 'hard' result, here is what John says in an e-mail to me about the long-term personal benefit from these insights:

"As I told you, what I took away from my Intensive is an acknowledgement of my own 'baggage'—stuff that I didn't even know I was carrying! When I confronted that, it was just *lifted from me*. It took me time to re-program myself—I am always working on it, but it gets easier. Having the weight off my shoulders made the re-programming so much less difficult.

"One thing I notice now, five and a half years after my Intensive, is that for the first 18-24 months, I thought about my baggage *every day*. Not with resentment, but just reconciling so many things in my life, re-ordering what is important. After a while I started getting down on myself about still thinking about it. 'Come on, John, it's time to move on!' I realize now that I was falling back on the old game—beating up on myself. However, at some point, it just stopped. One day the old baggage crossed my mind and I realized how long it had been since I had thought about it. Isn't that great!? I realize now it was just a healing period, something I had to go through, and I came out the other side. Now I can say with complete honesty that I have become more myself and I like who I have become. For anyone who hasn't yet gotten to that place, let me tell you, it's a short, cliché-like sentence—'I know and like who I am'—but it changes *everything.*"

He ended his note to me with these words:

"Now, John Scherer, I am going to close this e-mail, since my eyes are filling up with tears. Use this any way you want if it works for you, or just pass if it doesn't fit. You have an important message and people need to hear it. Feel free to use my name if you want—I have no problem with that. So, from that special place in my heart that you helped me find ... I send my love to you and your team."

As it is to most people, John's wake-up call was a surprise to him. He hadn't realized what was happening. It's a shame, because the world is constantly giving us feedback about how our life is working, but we often fail to take notice. So life, or the universe, has to hit us with a bigger stick, and it will keep hitting us until we stop and take notice. The same thing happens with organizations. The marketplace is a continuous, real-time feedback mechanism, sending signals to your organization about how it's doing. Losing membership or market share, high employee turnover, and bankruptcy—like illness and death for individuals—is simply feedback at the most extreme level.

Your task as an adult is to come to understand the presence and impact of your Somebody Training and how it has been running your life, so as to have a chance to go beyond it. You might be ready to start transcending your early programming, unleashing yourself into a more fulfilling and effective way of being and working in the world. The first step is to accept and appreciate your Somebody Training Faculty Members for their loving intent, and then get about breaking your old patterns using the third of the FIVE QUESTIONS: WHAT RUNS ME?

Discovering What Runs You

Your family of origin Faculty trained you to be a certain kind of person through your Somebody Training. That training 'took' and has evolved over the years into your Autopilot, your automatic, habitual way of thinking, feeling, and operating. *That's* what has been running you. Your own personal operating system, created in your Somebody Training. Now it's time to explore the nuts and bolts of this routine that has been running your life. To accomplish this, we'll be using a concept I developed in 1987 called Peeling the Onion. The theory behind this model is that, like the onion, you have many layers, leading down into a core at the center. By peeling back these layers, you will begin to see more clearly just what runs you, at home and at work.

The Persona

In the days of the ancient Greek Theater, actors on stage used masks, held on sticks. (The smiling and frowning thespian symbols associated today with the theater are reminders of this old prop.) By using multiple masks, a single actor (always male) could play two or three roles by holding up different masks as he spoke his lines. The actor, standing behind the mask, delivered his lines *through* the mask, making it possible for the audience to know which character was speaking and how to relate to him. The masks also portrayed varying emotions and showed clearly whether the character portrayed was a man or a woman. It's more than interesting that the Greek word for that mask was *persona,* from which we get our concepts like *person* and *personality.* The important thing to get is that the audience was relating to the *mask* and not the actor behind the mask.

It's the same today. As a result of your own Somebody Training, you have developed your own special 'social mask' or Persona, which you aim outward toward your world. You might think of yourself as on a stage, holding your Persona in front of you, showing the audience what you want them to see—and hiding what you don't want them to see. Picture a life-size blow-up of you, kept full of air with a hand pump. As you look out at the people around you from behind the doll, you often pump like crazy to keep the full-length shape in front of you as big as you can get it. *Are they buying it? you wonder. Better pump some more!*

Peeling The Onion

Here's how to find out what your own Persona looks like:

Step 1

Imagine that the diagram inset is an onion with the outer layer (the one to the far right) being those aspects of yourself you *want* the world to see.

Step 2

To generate an image of your Persona characteristics and qualities, ask yourself these questions:

Persona

Bright & quick
Vital
Compassionate
Lean
A Good Person
Salvific (way beyond helpful)
Insightful
Exciting
Courageous
Warm
Open-minded
Sensitive
Strong
Resourceful
Fun & funny
Spiritually Alive
Articulate
Persuasive
Knows everything

⋄ Who are three people—from history, literature, or your own life—whom I admire or love? What words would I use to describe the traits I admire most about them?

⋄ What kind of person am I *supposed* to be?

⋄ What kind of person am I *trying* to be?

⋄ What words would I hope people would use if they talked about me?

Step 3

As these words come to you, write them down along the outer line. (Some of them ought to feel a little embarrassing, but true. Put them down anyway.)

Step 4

Take a few moments to look over the words you have written. Each one has a story behind it. Whether or not you can remember it, each quality or characteristic is on your Persona list because of a teaching/learning moment from your Somebody Training. Think about who or what caused that word to show up on your Persona list.

Step 5

Now circle the three or four qualities and characteristics you would most like to hold on to or would be most reluctant to give up. If you could only retain three or four, which ones would you keep? For me they would be the ones in bold: Insightful, Vital, Spiritually Alive, and Good Person.

Step 6

What character from literature, history, movies, or television epitomizes some or all of these traits? You are looking for someone who can serve as a kind of *icon* for you. If you 'click' on this character, the world of some of those qualities opens up beneath them. My Persona Character Icon is The Eagle Scout, the one for others, a model boy/man.

In the FIVE QUESTIONS seminars, Persona Characters have included:

Superman	John Wayne	Moses
Mother Teresa	Oprah	Princess Di
Abraham Lincoln	Xena, Warrior Princess	Hercules

Albert Einstein	The Buddha	Hillary
Maya Angelou	Bill Clinton	JFK
Christopher Reeve	Charlie Brown	Nelson Mandela
Wonder Woman	Florence Nightingale	Joan of Arc

Sometimes it is not a person but a powerful phrase that will grab you. One Toronto woman, looking for an image that captured the sense of having to be the complete female, including the perfect body, the perfect wife, mother, and community volunteer, chose The Package. The character might turn out to be a simple phrase that resonates with you, like Brave Leader or Wise One or The Hero.

Notice What You Notice: The Power Of The Persona*

Your Persona is more than a clever concept. It works on you all day long. When you walk into a room, *notice what it is that you notice* about everyone there. You may find yourself noticing who is attractive, or who looks 'safe', or who seems to have power or status. *What you notice is not random.* It is no accident that you notice what you notice. Your Persona, and the various 'currencies' it works with, are shaping what you see.

Remember the carpet expert and the electrician in Chapter Four? We notice what we have been trained to notice. Makes you wonder what is being missed.

When I walk into a room 'on automatic' with my Eagle Scout Persona activated, I notice (without thinking) who needs help, what problems are present that need fixing by my clever, quick, vital resourcefulness. I may not even be aware that I am noticing these things, but as long as I am unconscious about my Persona being 'on', I

---

* 'Notice what you notice' is a wonderful concept from my friend and colleague, Ted Buffington. www.toachieve.com

will find myself, in conversations with people, listening for—and hearing—issues they are facing and problems that need solving, *even if they are not actually talking about them.* That's the point. *You are seeing what your Persona is primed to look for.* In order for your Persona character to have remained in place for so long, you have, again unconsciously, created a drama, a play, within which your role 'works.'

If you were to write a play with your Persona Character in the main role, who or what *else* would you have to write into the script? What other characters need to be 'on stage' for the play to move along, allowing your Persona to stay in character?

For my Eagle Scout Persona to 'work' I would need in the script:

⋄ people who need help or have a problem to solve—and who are willing to let me help them.

⋄ others who are less capable than I am, so I can be 'the one' who is special, The Eagle Scout.

⋄ fellow Scouts, helping as many people as possible.

⋄ merit badges, ways to show off my prowess at mastering the many areas and levels of ability.

⋄ proud parents, and loving others who give their praise and appreciation for the wonderful work I am doing.

⋄ challenging situations which allow me to bring forth my resourceful cleverness.

My friend, Mark, whose Persona is Sir Galahad, needs to have in his script:

- damsels in distress who need rescuing. (When Mark sees a woman crying, for instance, he will be right there in a nanosecond, usually equipped with a Kleenex.™)

- dragons that need slaying. (These might be forces in a situation that are threatening people, or issues like the environment, or individuals who are preying on more helpless people.)

- other knights to be better than—or more virtuous than. (When Mark is in his Persona, it is important to Mark to look good compared to any other 'knights' in the room.)

- kings and people in high places to hang with and to champion his work. (In his chosen work as a leadership coach and consultant, he often finds himself in the presence of senior executives who need and appreciate his help.)

- flexible but strong armor and great weapons. (Mark and I joke about how he is able to come out of a skirmish unscathed and 'right' about the issues, having turned the tables on the attacker and smoothly caused the other person to lose the 'joust.')

Another colleague, Lynnea, whose Persona is Wonder Woman, often finds herself in a special kind of drama along with:

- villains who need to be put in their place. (These might be people in an organization she is consulting with who are doing damage to their co-workers, or even drivers on the road who break the law or throw trash out the window.)

⬧ many complex situations that demand her attention. (Her life is loaded with people and relationships, all of which seem to need a lot of her attention, taxing her super-powers to the limit.)

⬧ a band of other Amazons who inhabit a 'secret island', a sisterhood. (Lynnea has a special group of mostly women she meets with regularly who support her in this work and who, themselves, play similar roles in their situations.)

⬧ an older sidekick (Captain What's-His-Name) who knows and respects who she really is and works alongside her, providing crucial assistance and linkage to the 'official' world in her Super Hero efforts. (I and several other colleagues of hers have played this role in her life and work.)

⬧ bracelets for deflecting bullets and a lariat that makes people tell the truth. (Lynnea has an amazing ability to gracefully parry accusations or criticism as if she were protected by an invisible shield—or magic bracelets. She also has a way of getting people to tell the truth about what is going on, insisting on it actually, in her work as a consultant and executive coach.)

One executive chose Hannibal, the great Carthaginian General from the Third Century BCE (not the scary movie character played by Anthony

Hopkins). He saw immediately how he turned everyone and everything around him into one of these:

   ⋄   an army of loyal, committed followers. (He had a reputation for engendering amazingly high levels of devotion among his employees.)

   ⋄   an enemy to be vanquished. (He said he saw potential enemies everywhere he looked, whose presence actually inspired him to maximum creativity and effort.)

   ⋄   mountains like the Alps to be climbed. (He got bored in a job unless there were huge challenges to be overcome. If there weren't any, he saw how he *created* them, "to make things interesting," he confessed.)

   ⋄   a kingdom, way back there somewhere, that wanted him to conquer the world. (He liked to operate away from headquarters, out in the trenches and on the front lines, where the battle for market share was taking place.)

Remember, almost all this is going on beneath your level of awareness as you are unconsciously trapped in the drama. This is important. If someone shows up on the stage of your life who is not willing or able to play one of the roles available, they just won't fit in. They will eventually fall off the stage of your life, or you will boot them off. You will find another job or line of work, or another spouse or partner, or you will fire them.

This Persona Drama is also important because, in your tendency to turn people and events into what you need them to be, you are highly likely to miss whatever *else* might be present. Remember that Default World diagram in Chapter Five, illustrating why we do what we do? You will *see* what is around you in terms of your drama—and miss whatever else is there. As The Eagle Scout, I am likely to notice what needs to be fixed and miss how okay things actually are, as well as the helpful gifts present in the other people there. Sir Galahad will tend to see the damsel as needing to be rescued and miss how she is actually doing fine, just having a sad moment. Wonder Woman will see yet another Superhero task to be added to the list of things she needs to take on, and miss how she could relax and let someone else pick up the gauntlet this time. Hannibal misses and possibly diminishes the true leadership qualities in those around him in his quest to be the world conqueror.

Your Persona Icon, like the icons on your computer screen, represents an entire set of programs and routines beneath them. Like computer programs, your Persona also took a lot of programming to make it easy to access. 'Click' on your Persona Icon—which happens all the time—and this program, written during your Somebody Training, comes alive, helping you see what you need to see and do what you need to do. As long as you remain unconscious about all this, you don't have a Persona; it has you.

I would like to propose that you have maxed out on your Persona, that you can't go where you want to go next with your life by shining or pumping up your Persona any more. What you need is just a little of someone *else* who lives inside you, someone a lot more frightening, and about whom you have a lifetime of negative programming. It just happens, however, to be exactly what the doctor ordered: your Shadow.

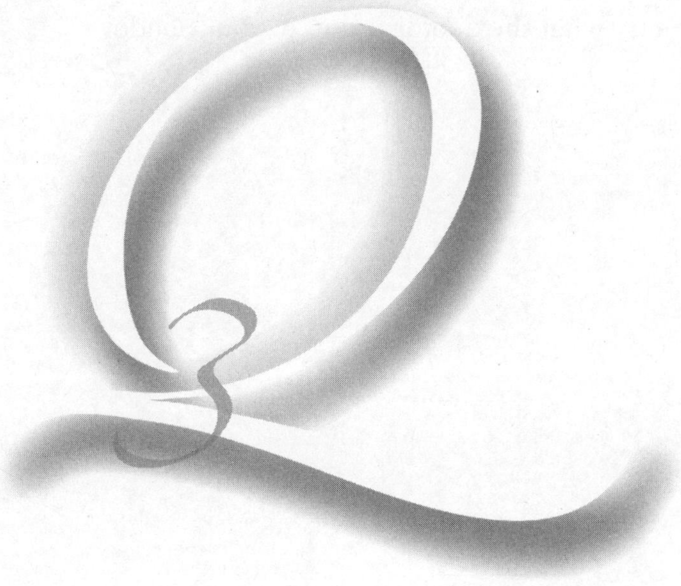

Chapter Eight

The Shadow Knows

There is a good reason your Persona has lasted so long. Your Somebody Training also included admonitions, sometimes even dire warnings, *not* to be certain things. One of two things probably happened. One or both parents may have received an admonition in *their* Somebody Training, which they felt must be passed on to you, or you may have done something that made your parents nervous, something they had to correct or 'nip in the bud.' (My mother's letter to my grandfather contained several perfect examples of this, like, *We can't let Johnny think he can get what he wants.*)

Every exhortation to *be* a certain way implies that there is also a way you should *not* be. If you are supposed to be <u>nice</u>, then you must *not* be _____ (fill in the blank). If you're supposed to be <u>strong</u>, then it's crucial that you *not* be _____, etc., etc.

Following the same process used in discovering the Persona, here's a simple way to find out what your Shadow looks like.

What I am NOT!	*What I am!*
Shadow/NOT	**Persona**
Mean	Bright & quick
Vicious	**Vital**
Destructive	Compassionate
Self-absorbed	Lean
Materialistic	***A Good Person***
Bigoted	Salvific (way beyond helpful)
Dogmatic	**Insightful**
Imperious	Exciting
Lazy	Courageous
Slow on the uptake	Warm
Grim or heavy	Open-minded
Insensitive	Sensitive
Cold	Strong
Calculating	Resourceful
Helpless	Fun & funny
A Whiner	**Spiritually Alive**
Emotionally Explosive	Articulate
	Persuasive
	Knows everything
Bobby Knight	***The Eagle Scout***

| *My Shadow Icon* | *My Persona Icon* |

Step 1:   *Identify the traits.*

My shadow icon represents those aspects of myself that I would NOT want the world to see me as. Ask yourself these questions:

- ◇ Who are three people—from history, literature, or my own life—whom I hate or despise? What words would I use to describe the traits I hate or despise most about them?
- ◇ What kind of person am I *NOT supposed* to be?
- ◇ What kind of person am I *trying NOT* to be?
- ◇ What words would I hope people would NOT use if people talked about me?

Write down the words that come to you along the inner arc, as I have on my own Onion.

Step 2:   *Probe each word's history.*

As you did with your Persona, take a few moments to look over the words you have written down for your Shadow. Each word has a story behind it. Each quality, trait, or characteristic is on your Shadow list because of some teaching moment from your Somebody Training.

Step 3:   *Highlight the worst traits.*

Now highlight the three or four words that, when you are truly honest with yourself, are the worst ones on the list, the ones that you would let go of first if you could? (For me they are Destructive, Emotionally Explosive, Arrogant, and Imperious: "Do what I say because I say so. My way is the only way.")

Step 4: *Select your Shadow Icon/Character.*
What character from literature, history, movies, or
television epitomizes some or all of these most negative
traits? You might simply think of someone you despise,
someone you would never want to be like. You are
looking for someone who can serve as another *Icon* for
you, so that whenever you 'click' on this character, the
most important of your Shadow traits are represented.
(My Shadow Icon recently has been Bobby Knight, the
highly successful college basketball coach also known
for throwing chairs during games, yelling at referees,
and berating his players.)

In recent Five Questions seminars Shadow Icons
have included:

Hillary	Charlie Brown	Angelica (*Rugrats*)
Leona Helmsley	J.R. Ewing	Adolf Hitler
Bill Clinton	Judas	Alexis (*Dallas*)
Saddam Hussein	The Devil	Dennis Rodman
Howard Stern	Osama Bin Laden	Margaret Thatcher
G. W. Bush	Cruella deVille	Wicked Stepmother
Timothy McVeigh	Dilbert	The Emperor (*Star Wars*)

Just as with your Persona, it may not be a person from
history or a literary character, but a powerful phrase
that captures the essence of your Shadow. My friend,
Mark Yeoell, a brilliant leadership coach and facilitator,
in looking for a character that epitomized a brutish,
violent, take-no-prisoners approach to life, chose The
Way Men Are. A highly successful entrepreneur friend
of mine found a character that for him embodied

manipulation, self-centeredness, and sleaze: the Used Car Salesman. Just make sure that whatever you write in that box resonates in your heart and soul as a perfect label for what you would hate to think was in you.

The Persona tends to drive us in positive ways, while the Shadow drives us *away* from certain behaviors and situations. Just as the Eagle Scout looks for situations where he can be helpful and impressive, my reluctance to be Bobby Knight has me avoiding people and places where there could be explosive emotional outbursts. My concern about being hurtful sometimes stops me from standing tall in my own truth or expressing my feelings at times when that is precisely what is called for.

My colleague, Tricia Karpfen, herself a seminar leader of amazing skill and sensitivity, chose Leona Helmsley as her Shadow Icon. For Tricia, calling attention to herself is a bad thing, which she avoids like the plague. In learning to deliver our seminars, she worked hard on developing her capacity to stand in front of a group of people and speak forcefully, or act as if she had something to say worth listening to. Being a Leona, with all the attention-getting, self-absorbed things that went with her, was so awful to Tricia that she still finds it a little challenging to wear makeup or jewelry that might be seen as ostentatious.

Another colleague, Lynnea, trying hard *not* to be a Dilbert, occasionally has trouble admitting that she is not on top of something, even when that would be a natural and expected response.

Meet the Parents

This Shadow character didn't come into the world without *parents*. Very early on in life, you and I learned in our Somebody Training what was 'good' and what was 'bad.' What brought us good feelings or results and what brought us bad feelings or results. Our Persona and Shadow characters both were born out of that union of pleasure and pain. Let's now *meet the parents*.

Chapter Nine

The Addiction
and the Terror

What has kept your Autopilot going for so long,
years after its development in your childhood?
Psychologists have known since the turn of the
Nineteenth Century—and the spiritual masters for
many thousands of years—that what motivates us as
human beings is a combination of seeking Pleasure and
avoiding Pain. Pavlov's dogs learned to go for what gave
them food, and avoid what gave them a mild shock. B.F.
Skinner applied this principle to humans and found
that we, too, operate much like Pavlov's dogs, only
dressed up a little differently. In organizations, the field
of Performance Management—how to get people to
do what they are supposed to do—is based on similar
assumptions. Here is a crash course on a few of the
fundamental principles of Performance Management,
as explained to me by my colleague, Jesse Watson,
himself a pioneer in the field.

❖ *What gets rewarded, gets repeated.* When your Somebody Training Faculty wanted you to do something, they rewarded you when you did it. To work best, the reward needed to be Positive, Immediate, and Concrete (or PIC, pronounced 'pick' in the Performance Management trade). The reinforcement that worked best gave you a reward right away in a 'currency' that was important to you. Telling you that you were special when what you really wanted was a hug it would not have worked.

❖ *What gets punished or ignored is less likely to happen often.* Sometimes your faculty gave you a Negative Immediate Concrete response to what you did (a NIC in the jargon): sharp words, a scowl, a spanking, or withholding something you wanted. Even negative feedback is *attention,* and some little ones craved attention so much they developed clever strategies for getting their Faculty to punish them. Sometimes the only way to get someone to stop doing something is to ignore the behavior altogether.

Your Somebody Training faculty provided just the right balance of PICs and NICs to shape you into who you have become, most likely without even realizing they were doing it. Most parents are not consciously trying to manipulate their children into becoming a certain kind of person, although I am sure you have observed what *looked* like this from time to time. In your case, it just happened as a result of the way they interacted with you from day to day. When you did something they liked, they either said so directly or gave some subtle sign that it was a good thing, like a warm smile. Likewise, when you did something they didn't like, you probably got a clear message of their displeasure, like a frown. That little person—you—figured out very early what the game was and who you needed to *be* and what you needed to *do* to get the 'goody', whether it was love or attention or control or privacy or respect or whatever you thought you needed. Just think: you figured all this out before the age of five!

Here's the key point: *You are still operating as if you need (and don't have) that goody.* Unless you have done a lot of deep inner/ spiritual development work on yourself, you are still walking around at the effect of that early programming, moving instinctively *toward* people and situations that will get you what you are instinctively seeking, and *away from* people and situations that might get you what you are instinctively afraid of and want to avoid. By this time in your life, these two drivers have turned into things so powerful and unconscious that I want to turn up the heat and call them by name:

⬦ your Addiction

⬦ your Terror

You may want to argue with me about this re-naming but, trust me, these two forces live in you exactly that way.

Fill in the two boxes on the left (inner) side of The Onion with what you are Seeking (Addiction) and Avoiding (Terror). Here's what mine are:

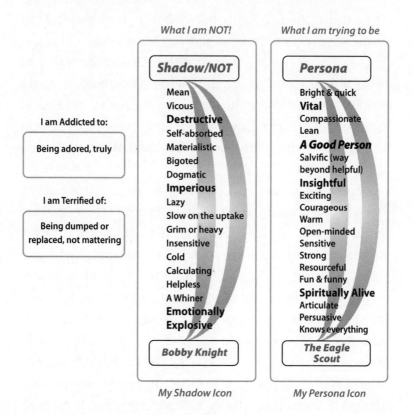

My Shadow Icon   My Persona Icon

TEWA: *Locked On And Tracking*

Here's how powerful these two drivers are. During our Somebody Training, we develop an amazing radar, as my own personal development coach, Jan Smith, calls it, capable of detecting potential threats from far away. This is more than a metaphor for me.

For four years I served as Combat Officer and Air Controller on a destroyer in the US Navy. In that role, one of my jobs was called TEWA (Threat Evaluation and Weapon Assignment), making recommendations to the Captain or the Officer of the Deck on the bridge to help 'fight the ship.' To assist us, we had sensors for keeping track of what was happening in the air and in the sea around us. While our old SPS-6 and SPS-10 radars didn't work like they were supposed to some of the time, we were able to do a pretty good job of staying on top of what was coming at us. Whenever our radar detected an inbound unidentified aircraft, we designated it as a 'bogey', gave it a number, and began to track it. My job was to prioritize all the threats coming at us and make a recommendation to the Captain which weapon system we should use to defend ourselves, if it came to that.

Fortunately for us, we never had to confront a hostile enemy bogey. The Combat Officer aboard *USS Vincennes* a few years back, patrolling in the Persian Gulf, wasn't so lucky. Based on the information he had in the 120 seconds or so he had available to make the TEWA decision, he recommended shooting at what appeared to be a hostile jet aircraft coming directly at them from Iranian airspace, flying a text-book Exocet anti-ship missile-launching profile. As it turned out, the height-finding radar information given to him was *inverted,* meaning the radar operator interpreted the jet as *descending*—as an attacking plane would be— when, in fact, it was actually *climbing*. Later, it became clear that the aircraft was an off-course commercial airliner whose identification equipment was either faulty or turned off. The downing of a civilian airplane with hundreds of innocent passengers became another tragic international incident.

Blood in the water

For our purposes, however, it serves as a dramatic reminder of what can happen when we make decisions concerning what is 'coming at us.' These kinds of TEWA decisions are repeated many times a day in your life, thankfully without the tragic loss of innocent lives. Whenever you 'walk into a room' (I use this phrase to represent your entering any life situation), your radar is in *search mode,* constantly but usually unconsciously scanning the room for any signs of both what you are seeking (or addicted to) and what you are trying to avoid (your terror). Like the shark, which can detect one part per trillion of blood in the water at great distances, your radar can pick up the slightest indicator that you might be running the risk of experiencing what you are desperate to avoid.

For me it means wanting people to see me as an awesome, spiritually alive man, capable of facilitating life changing transformation during even a simple conversation. Let's say an important client of mine suddenly remembers a tough phone call they have to make and pulls a face while we are talking. If I am not awake and aware, my default impulse—triggered by my Autopilot—will be to assume it has something to do with *me.* My mind will start to replay what transpired just before he made the face in an attempt to figure out what I need to do to bring him back to a positive evaluation of me. Without any conscious thought, I will find myself saying or doing something to impress him, to 'get him back', and will keep up this act until the danger signals recede.

Sounds bizarre, doesn't it? It sure does as I read it. Yet that is exactly what happens off and on all day every day as long as you are on Autopilot. Until you become conscious and aware of the pattern—and take steps to change the way you process your life—you are walking around as a reactive, interpretive machine, angling for as many 'hits' of what you are addicted to as possible, and avoiding like the plague what you are terrified of. And it's all unconscious.

So, when I am on Autopilot, I am going around 'scoring' as many little hits of Adoration and Respect as I can, and avoiding anything that might get me Replaced or Dumped or Not Mattering. Whenever I am able to turn a potential Dumping into Adoration, then my Autopilot tells me I've *really* done something worth celebrating! When that happens, I can finally rest internally for, oh, several *seconds* before I have to crank up the old Routine again and sally forth to score some more Adoration.

The Con

This might hurt a little, but can you see how this whole way of being is actually a kind of Con? Remember that the term 'con man' comes from the word *confidence*. A confidence man/woman is: *a)* attempting to gain your confidence, by *b)* pretending/trying to be someone you will trust, so c) they can get what they want from you, d) without your realizing you're in their 'game' and being 'had.' If that isn't what most of we human beings are doing all day, every day, I don't know what is!

We are walking around pretending to be _____ _____ (fill in the blank from your Persona), so we can score little hits of _____ (fill that in from your Addiction) without other people realizing that that's the real game, regardless of what appears to be the topic of conversation. We are constantly—usually unconsciously—angling for our Addiction, but not wanting anyone to see what we are up to. Heck, we don't even want to see it ourselves!

I hope you can sense the irony at work here. This is no way to live, is it? Yet, it is what passes as life for many of us much of the time. Fortunately, there is a way to wake up and change the game. With practice—lots of it—it is possible to turn Automatic Living (that is, *what runs you*) into Authentic Living, full of a profound sense of satisfaction and deep purpose, something beyond looking good to score your addiction and avoid your terror. I will show you how to shift your state from automatic to authentic in discussing the fifth of the Five Questions: What Will Unleash Me?

The Autopilot Summary

Here are the Cliff Notes® of what we have explored so far:

⋄ When you were born, you became enrolled in the local Somebody Training school—your family of origin.

- ◇ The people around you—parents, siblings, aunts and uncles, teachers, scoutmasters, coaches, even neighbors—were your Faculty.

- ◇ They did their best to help you turn into the kind of Somebody that could make it in the world.

- ◇ They helped you develop a sense of who you are, complete with clothes, a self-concept, certain skills and qualities for you to *portray* to the rest of the world—and to yourself—which became your Persona.

- ◇ As you matured, you polished and added skills and qualities to this Persona, and it has served you well, getting you to this point in your life.

- ◇ Your Faculty also helped you develop a healthy resistance to certain other ways of being that were deemed to be wrong or bad or would in some way detract from your ability to make it in the world—which became your Shadow.

- ◇ Unbeknownst to them, their 'curriculum' also developed in you a sense of what you were missing or wished you had more of—which became your Addiction.

- ◇ It also developed in you a fear of experiencing something else, something so damaging (at least in your young mind) that it must be avoided at all costs—which became your Terror.

- ◇ When you 'walk into a room', unless you are conscious and aware of what is happening, this automatic way of living becomes who you 'are' from moment to moment—your Autopilot.

❖ It all adds up to your Con of which you have been blissfully unaware—until now. Sorry, but there you have it.

At this point, you may be feeling a little depressed, or doubtful. Keep reading, because there is Good News, Bad News, and Even Better News.

Chapter Ten

Good News, Bad News, and Even Better News

The Good News: *Every one of those traits, qualities, and characteristics that you put down on your Persona list **is in you right now.***

If they weren't present to some extent, they would have dropped off your list by now. You can't fake your Persona, at least not for long. If a certain quality you are trying to portray isn't in you—at least a little—the feedback you have received would have extinguished it as a possibility. If you're still trying to *be* it, it's *in you now.* If you see it in someone else, it's in you first. As Intensive graduate Sandy Pierce said it: "If you spot it, you got it." (Remember that when you look out at the world, you are seeing it in terms of your own history.)

It's really *you* in there, back behind the projected image, actually *being* all those things you are *trying* or pretending to be. Isn't that ironic? Here you are, walking around all day every day, trying or pretending to be something that you simply *are!* So, relax. Quit trying so hard to make your Persona 'work.' When you 'walk into a room', guess who walks in? It's the real you, complete with all those characteristics you listed in your Persona.

You don't have to *try* so hard to be bright or clever or inspirational. Sometimes you just *are*—and, of course, sometimes you're not.

Having a Persona is not a bad thing; it's a human thing. What makes the Persona a problem is your constant effort to *do* a particular quality, like Authentic or Vital or Insightful. My personal development coach, Jan Smith, drilled me once, "John, you know how to *do* 'authentic' better than anyone I know!" Stop *trying* to be a certain kind of person made up of all good qualities. Instead, simply trust that each of your naturally present Persona qualities will come forward when it is required. Remember: You don't have to change yourself; you need to be *become* yourself—that will change everything.

You already *are* who you are trying to be, *so just become more fully who that is.* This means you can get on with your life, bringing every one of your highly developed Persona skills and well-honed qualities to more important missions, as you will see. What if all those gifts were all put in the service of something more fulfilling and more significant than trying to make you look good? But we are getting ahead of ourselves.

The Bad News

You guessed it—The Bad News is that whatever you put on your Shadow list, the things you say you are *not*— as in "I am NOT _____ (fill in the blank)"—is also actually very much alive in you. So is what you hate in other people. This is called Projection, a principle of Gestalt psychology. When you see something you hate in someone else, you are seeing 'bad' stuff that is in you. Since it is 'bad', it *can't* be in <u>you</u>. The mind resolves that tension by locating it (projecting it) 'out there' onto someone else.

Another interesting thing about Shadow material is that since it is being denied—"That's not in me!"—it leaks out in inappropriate ways. As you will see, when you don't acknowledge and accept the presence of this Shadow aspect of who you are, like Anger, for instance, you will find yourself getting upset about trivial stuff, leaving people to wonder: "What the heck was that all about?!"

If your Shadow was Hitler and you had Destructive on your Shadow list, I'll grant that you are not destructive like Adolf Hitler was destructive, but you *are* destructive the way *you* are destructive. I guarantee that the people who know you best would be able to tell you—they probably won't, though—just what 'destructive' looks like in your case.

Sean: *I'm Not Lazy*

At Sean's Intensive, his question was: *How does Laziness live in me right now?* Laziness was on his Shadow list out of his dedication to not be like his father, who couldn't hold a job and mostly laid around the house, drinking. "No, sir," he said, "I'm not like that!"

When he looked carefully and without blame, though, he could smell the faint traces of laziness in his procrastination throughout his academic life, even manifesting itself today in his waiting until the last minute to prepare overheads for a presentation or putting off a challenging work assignment until he absolutely *had* to do it.. He smelled it in his reluctance to balance his checkbook and read his monthly spreadsheet as if it mattered. So, eventually, he saw it clearly: "*I am lazy* at times about certain things. Meanwhile, I walk around telling myself that I am *not* lazy (like my father) because I work hard to generate income for my family and I get up and go to work every day. That kind of unconscious self-righteousness makes it hard for me to be compassionate toward people I label as lazy. It also makes it really hard for me to relax and take care of myself."

So, you now have The Good News and The Bad News. You are going to love The Even Better News.

The Even Better News

So, the Good News is that everything you are trying or pretending to be with your Persona, you already are, so you can relax and just trust that whatever is called for by the situation will come out of you when it is needed. The Bad News is that every single one of the Shadow qualities you said you were *not* is also present in you.

The Even Better News is that there are nuggets of pure gold buried in your Shadow—in that 'bad stuff' you have denied—waiting to be uncovered, refined, and put to use in your life. I call them Stretches because they take you beyond where you are now—and increase your 'range' as a human being.

Here are two applications:

First, every one of your Shadow qualities, which you have thrown out like old bath water, actually contains an incredibly valuable and precious 'baby' which you need to reclaim and eventually even embrace. Each Shadow characteristic reveals essential clues on how to take your life to the next level of purpose, power, and peace. In a moment, I am going to show you how to get from a negative Shadow characteristic to the very powerful and positive Transformational Stretch.

Second, you may not like to hear this, but *your Shadow Character has a lot to teach you,* and you will not be able to get very far along in your development without profound learning from this surprising and possibly disgusting new teacher. It's time to *un*-learn a few lessons from your Somebody Training and 'go to school' with someone you disrespect, despise, or even hate. That person you can't stand can become a new Faculty member even more important to your present than your original teachers, because he or she is going to be helping you get some crucial lessons you missed the first time around.

In the sections that follow, you will learn how to take your Shadow Character and the words that went along with it and find in the ugly something beautiful, in the repulsive something you desperately need. Remember, you don't need to *change* yourself; you need to *become* yourself. One of the most powerful things you can do in that regard is to tackle what comes next: discovering the life-enhancing, transformational Stretches embedded in your Shadow Character and in your Shadow Characteristics—the things you are *not*.

Chapter Eleven

Life Transforming Muscle in Your Shadow

If your development into the person you are capable of being is not about *changing* yourself, but *becoming* yourself, where can you go to take a step in that direction? You do not need more Persona. Consider that you may have maxed out from counting on your Persona. What you need in order to go to the next level of self-development is in your Shadow, in precisely what you are *not*. Your Autopilot is programmed to resist any hint of these negative labels, but inside each of those terrible Shadow characteristics is a 'muscle' you desperately need to stretch and strengthen to become a more complete and effective human being.

The thought of looking for something of positive value in your Shadow Character may, however, be a frightening prospect to you. The Shadow is, after all, made up of things you have been under strong admonitions *not* to be, with the promise of terrifying consequences if you let even a little of it out. In its effort to protect you from your Terror (*e.g.* Being Dumped or Rejected or Dismissed) your Autopilot/Con stops you from even *getting onto the continuum* of any Shadow characteristic.

Sean Revisited

One of Sean's Shadow qualities, mentioned above, was Ruthless. Can you see that Ruthlessness, which is a bad thing, is actually too much of something that, at the right time and place, could be a good thing? For instance, what do you get if you put Ruthlessness on a kind of rheostat with a knob that will allow you to turn its intensity up and down? What if you could turn *down* Ruthlessness with your rheostat (but not turn it *off*) until it became something that would not only be okay, but would even be *crucial* to your development into the complete human being that you are becoming?

Here's how it could work:

As you can see, as Sean turns down the intensity on Ruthless (a Deadly No-No in his Somebody Training), it first becomes Mean, then Selfish (which is still not okay). As he keeps reducing its badness, it becomes Demanding (which is sort of okay), then it becomes Assertive (which is on the borderline of being a 'good' thing for him), then finally it becomes Clear About What I Want, which is *crucial to his effectiveness and fulfillment*. A fully functional human being *must* have access to strength and clarity from time to time!

For Sean, though, this whole continuum of options was collapsed. He couldn't tell one end from the other.

Crucial	Sort of OK	Not OK	Deadly No-No
No Problem Well within tolerance. Not Risky. In fact it is *essential* to effectiveness and a sense of fulfillment.	Mostly acceptable Low risk. Probably Ok to do safely.	Increasingly risky. Feels scary and threatening to the Adaptive Routine.	Dangerous To be avoided at all cost. 'Guaranteed' to bring on the feared consequence, the Terror

Strong & Clear — Assertive — Demanding — Selfish — Mean — Ruthless

The mind says THIS ...

...it is actually THIS ...

Being clear felt—to him—like ruthlessness. Here's what used to happen inside him every time he thought about telling his staff he wanted something done. He couldn't even get started. As his mind whispered, "Now would be a good time to tell the Staff that you want your new program launched by next Friday, regardless of the effort," his Autopilot/Con whispered in his other ear: "Sean, ... Don't even think about it. ... That would be you acting Ruthless. ... We wouldn't want that, now would we? ... You know what happens to everyone when you are ruthless."

Vicki

With her permission, let's take another example from a colleague, Vicki. At her Intensive, she identified Self-centered as one of the Shadow characteristics she was definitely *not* supposed to be. Her repulsion of Self-centeredness meant that she often felt taken advantage of by the people she was serving, *i.e.* her children, her boss, her companions, even relative strangers. As a result, she occasionally felt depleted, resentful, and unappreciated. Once she realized that buried within Self-centeredness is the life-transforming stretch of Self-*nurturing*, Vicki has been able to live in a more balanced way and has since been caring for those she loves in ways that also feed her, while taking into account her own needs. "I still fall back into my old habit from time to time, but now I know that's what I am doing. I catch myself doing it. This process is a blessing and a curse! From now on, I will not be able to run my old game anymore without being aware that's what I am doing."

> Note: *It is very important that you not turn the 'bad' word into something positive and opposite.* Notice that, for Vicki, Self-centered didn't turn into Kind! She already had plenty of that in her Persona; she didn't need any more kindness. She needed Self-nurturing, something that was *not* in her comfortable repertoire, something that came from one of her Shadow Characteristics. So keep the essence of each word as you move it across the continuum.

Here are a few examples to give you a sense of how this works. Start at the right with the Deadly No-No and see how the characteristic works its way back across to become a Crucial Stretch on the left. You don't have to fill in each step if the Stretch jumps out at you:

My effectiveness could
increase as I have the
courage to ...

Up to now, I have been
afraid of being ...

Crucial Stretch	Sort of Okay	Not Okay	Deadly No-No
Be willing to admit I don't know	Out of it	Ignorant	Stupid
Relax and smell the roses			Lazy

| Let others lead sometimes | Out of it | Ignorant | Soft, Vulnerable |
| Take care of my own needs | | | Self-absorbed |

What Your Shadow Character Has to Teach You

Here comes that principle that may blow your mind: your Shadow Character needs to become your teacher—at least for a while—until you have integrated what he/she has to contribute to you. I can hear some of you already: "Are you serious? What could Adolf Hitler teach me?" Or how about Osama bin Laden or Leona Helmsley?

Emory, Meet Bill Clinton

At one of our seminars, Emory picked Bill Clinton as his Shadow, saying, as he did so, "What a jerk." (Bill Clinton also appears as a hero on many people's Persona Character list, by the way.) When I said to him, "You have a lot to learn from him, Emory!" he came unglued. He went into a tirade, yelling (I've cleaned it up a little here) that there was no way "that unethical slime-ball" had anything to teach him—or anybody—and threatened to walk out of the room. This may seem perverse, but I *love* it when something like this happens, because I know from experience that the more Emory hates Bill Clinton, the more his life will transform by opening to what Clinton has to teach him. When Emory was able to calm down and discover *in the hated character* the qualities and skills he was desperately missing, you could have heard a pin drop in that room.

Here's how it unfolded:

"Emory," I said, "squeeze out all of what you consider bad about Bill Clinton until you are left with the human being that he is, complete with all his gifts, skills and qualities. Okay, done that? Now, what is left in him that might be of great value to you, things you have not developed in yourself?"

"That guy has nothing to teach me! He's an immoral jerk. So don't even start trying to tell me there's anything useful for me in him!"

Several people in the group began to disagree and offered Emory some things to think about:

"Well, he's a great orator, articulate, clever. He knows how to work the crowd."

"Would 'working the crowd' be an okay thing for you, Emory?" I asked.

"Oh, yeah. ... Okay, that's a good thing. ... One I wish I had, actually. As a leader, I stand in the corner a lot and let others 'press the flesh' more than I should."

"What else?" I asked. People chimed in:

"Clinton knows how to build coalitions to get things done."

"He isn't afraid to go for big ideas and *sell* them to people."

Then Emory himself offered one: "Here's one: He snows people with bullshit."

"Emory!" I interrupted, "Keep it neutral, buddy."

"Okay. ... Busted. ... All right, he's charismatic and knows how to make complicated things easy for people to understand."

(Long pause.)

"Is that it?" I asked. "Gee, is that all Bill Clinton has going for him when you squeeze out everything that's 'bad'? Let's see. You said he is: articulate, bright, extremely well-informed, knows how to 'work the crowd', builds coalitions to get things done, isn't afraid to go for big ideas and sell them to people, is willing to fight for what he believes in, and can make really complicated things simple to understand. Now, Emory, how many of these traits and skills are ones that you know in your heart-of-hearts are missing or underdeveloped in *you* as a leader at work?"

(Another long pause as he thinks.)

"They all are, actually. ... Every single one of them."

"How badly do you need them? How crucial are they to the next phase of your life at home and at work?"

(Long pause, with some emotion coming to the surface.)

"Yeah. ... I really do need to be okay with standing for what I believe in, and building strong coalitions to accomplish my goals at work. I need to be more confident about going into a room full of strangers to make contacts. Bill Clinton's never met a stranger! This is amazing, John. ... I would never have guessed ..." His voice trailed off in wonder and amazement at what his hated Shadow character had to teach him. He had gone past the Good News and the Bad News to discover the Even Better News.

Chase: *Breakthrough For A Navy SEAL*

Chase sat quietly in his Intensive, interacting with his fellow participants, fully engaged, yet very much in the background. You might not have known he was in the room. From our conversation as part of his Pre-Work, however, I knew that he had been a member of highly-decorated Underwater Demolition Team 11 and SEAL Team One, serving several tours in Vietnam, receiving the Purple Heart and Bronze Star, with a Combat V. While he was 'in country' he was involved in firefights and barely escaped one ambush with his life, working under fire to help save members of his team. Chase was a true hero in the eyes of anyone who knows anything about the military world.

You would never have guessed his SEAL background. Quiet, mild-mannered, soft-spoken, it came as little surprise that, his Persona Character turned out to be Brian Picolo, the humble, but heroic football player. It was a perfect fit. His Shadow Character emerged as John McEnroe and he told us he couldn't stand what he saw as McEnroe's petulance, self-centeredness, uncontrollable anger, and meanness.

At one point Chase spoke hesitantly to the rest of the group in a voice barely audible: "Excuse me. ... Do you think it would be okay if I turned down the air conditioner? I mean, if not, that'd be okay, too. ..."

"Oh, I don't know ..." someone said playfully, "What do the rest of you think? Should we give Chase permission to turn down the air conditioner? Personally, I don't think we should. ..."

The whole group shouted things like, "No way!" "Absolutely not!"

"Oh, okay," Chase said at once, "I was just getting chilly ..."

"Chase," I asked, "how would John McEnroe handle this situation? Go to your Shadow for coaching."

After about a nanosecond, Chase stood up and blurted with great intensity, "Okay, guys! Listen up! I'm f- - - - -g freezing my ass off and I'm going to turn down the air conditioner. If anybody's got a problem with that, see me after the session." The smile on his face was deep and wide as he finished. "Man, that felt good!" he said, grinning at us all.

We all cheered and people slapped him on the back. You would have thought he had won the lottery. Actually, he had won a lot more than that. You see, in his role as a fundraiser for a statewide scholarship foundation, Chase had to call up and speak to very rich and important people, heads of large corporations, government officials, community leaders. After his John MacEnroe breakthrough, he revealed to us that stacks of telephone slips sat on his desk for weeks waiting for him to get past his fear of speaking to someone that 'big.' He admitted feeling almost nauseous as he sat pondering having to call these people to ask for their help, procrastinating much of the time, putting off making calls as long as possible.

All of us in the group were stunned. Here was a man who had undergone and passed the U.S. Navy's SEAL Program, the toughest, most harrowing psychological and physical winnowing in the world—training that only 1 in 1,000 come through successfully. SEALs have to confront armed and angry enemies on land, sea, and in the air. Imagine someone trained to sneak through the jungle after bad guys with a knife in his teeth being afraid of making a few phone calls! But that's exactly where he was. That's how powerful his Somebody Training and Autopilot had become for him.

In his resistance to ever again becoming that combat veteran with a knife in his teeth, Chase had thrown the baby out with the bath water. Because of his Terror of being Abandoned (what his Con told him would happen if he were ever to speak from his strength), Chase had lost the capacity to simply be clear and direct. In the process, however, he rediscovered a 'John McEnroe' alive and well inside him, the very same kind of determination, stubbornness, and courage that had enabled him to survive SEAL training and transcend his daily bouts with gut-wrenching fear as he fought his way through Vietnam kill zones. That same powerful, sometimes selfish, set of characteristics was exactly what he needed—again—to experience purpose, power, and peace.

On his return home, Chase reported to us that every time he had a tough phone call to make, he thought to himself, "Now, how would John MacEnroe handle this situation?" He then would take a breath, don his MacEnroe psyche, and make the call, usually with great delight and gusto. He told us that since that breakthrough, he has begun to actually look forward to these calls and has found people eager to help his cause. The Shadow knows ...

Eagle Scout, Meet Bobby Knight

My own Shadow Character has changed over the years as I have integrated different aspects of who I am *not* into my life, and reconnected with the creative power they had to contribute. For a while my Shadow was Saddam Hussein, representing my resistance to the self-absorbed use of power to dominate others. Studying him after squeezing out everything I saw as evil, my

Saddam Shadow taught me that it's okay:

- ⋄ to tell people what to do from time to time,

- ⋄ to be a person of significant influence, and

- ⋄ to relax more with outward symbols of status and power.

After that, my Shadow character was Jimmy Bakker, the TV evangelist. I have no doubt that he was a sensitive, spiritually alive man, but as an icon in the public eye, for some he had come to represent the sleazy, manipulative, self-absorbed guy who pretended to want to save your soul but, in reality, just wanted your money and your love. It took almost a year for me to see how Jimmy and I were alike, and then another year to transform what I had seen as sleazy manipulation into Stretches. Jimmy taught me how to:

- ⋄ communicate powerful, life changing messages to masses of people,

- ⋄ using an amazing variety of media, and

- ⋄ ask people for money to support something I believe in strongly.

I realized that to become a more complete John Scherer—and more effective in my work—I not only needed to hold on to what my Persona, the Eagle Scout, had to offer, but I also needed what Jimmy Bakker could teach me. Scouts know how to help people, usually one or two at a time, and how to stand with courage in the face of scary things in the 'woods' of life. Jimmy knew how to enroll millions of people in his vision, how to dream big, and how to use the media to create momentum. I'm still working on some of that.

Then a few years ago, in what could be called a 'dynamic conversation' with my wife, Catharine, in response to a question from her, I shared some things I saw in her that were hard for me to be around. The main one was what I called 'being emotionally out of control and explosive with rage.' Since the first step in transforming your *world* is to transform *your own inner life,* in this situation it meant shifting my weight from blame and 'building a case' against *her,* to taking on the very words I was using about her, and seeing how those things lived *in me.* I had to acknowledge that I was *looking at my own Shadow* when I saw her emotion and anger.

It didn't take any time at all for me to see where my reaction against 'being emotionally out of control and explosive with rage' came from. Since my father had been not only a gifted, delightful man, but also a fall-down drunk, I never brought a friend home from school for seventeen years, out of fear of what I would see when I opened the door at 3:30 p.m. He might be sitting there reading the newspaper, alive, vibrant, a delightful raconteur, genuinely eager to talk about my day, *or* he might be lying on the floor of the living room in his underwear amid the stench of old booze, stale cigarette smoke, and his own vomit, *or* he might start yelling at me with fire in his eyes and hate in his mouth for some mistake I had made but couldn't figure out. It was terrifying to come home in the afternoons, knowing that I might have to face the very real specter of Pop 'being emotionally out of control and explosive with rage.' There goes my Somebody Training at work again.

My friend suggested that I take this one on and see what it might lead to. I agreed, and thought, "Who would be a good Shadow Character that would epitomize for me unpredictable emotional volatility and explosiveness?" The answer came in seconds, Bobby Knight. (For readers not familiar with him, he is the basketball coach who went to Texas Tech after being fired as the basketball coach at Indiana University. The final straw was striking a freshman player during practice, a scene caught on video and replayed *ad nauseam* on the sports channels for weeks.) You might say that from time to time he demonstrated what could be called being emotionally out of control and explosive with rage. As he is portrayed in the media, Knight is known not only for being one of basketball's 'winningest' coaches, but also for yelling at his players and referees, throwing chairs and towels across the basketball court and, in general, being a loose cannon on the deck. I understand he has taken anger management classes and seems to have calmed down quite a bit.

One way to tell that you have the perfect Shadow Icon picked out is when you have an immediate negative reaction like the one I had at this point: "No way! That's not me! I would never be like him!" As I felt this resistance rising inside, I knew instinctively that he was the perfect choice. That kind of strong reaction meant he had a lot to teach me—if I had the courage to do the digging and learn some new behaviors from the best in my Shadow Character.

How To Discover What Your Shadow Character Has To Teach You

Step 1: List the bad qualities.

Make a list of all the things you find repulsive or unacceptable about your Shadow Icon. Don't soften it or make it politically correct. The more judgmental your words, the more powerful the insight to come. I developed a list for Bobby Knight and culled it down to the three most negative characteristics I saw in him:

⋄ Yelling and screaming, often directing it at people who were doing their best for him.

⋄ Acting as if his program were the only one that had validity. His attitude seemed to be, 'My way or the highway.'

⋄ Promoting winning at any cost, *driven* to beat the competition.

Step 2: Look for the Stretch.

Take each one and ask yourself, "What is the crucial, transformational *stretch* buried in this (unacceptable) behavior, something I truly *need* to become a more complete person at home and at work?" Here's what happened when I took a good, hard look at each of my three worst Bobby Knight characteristics and turned them into stretches:

⋄ 'Yelling and screaming' turned into *"John, you need to be more boldly expressive of how you feel, especially with your upsets."*

If I were to take this one on, it would mean that at times I would simply express my feelings and opinions, without running them through all the gates and check points to make sure no one's feelings might get hurt. Like telling a waiter when I really don't like the way my meal is prepared, or letting clients know when they do something that doesn't work for me. Since seeing this, I have actively looked for moments to practice being 'boldly expressive'—and this book is one of them!

⋄   'My way is the only way' became *"Honor and acknowledge the uniqueness and power of your work, John."*

In looking at this one, I realized that in my resistance to being a dogmatic fundamentalist, a 'true believer' not willing to be open to other paths to the truth (and there are a bunch of them in this field), I had leaned too far in the other direction.

At a recent seminar, a colleague said to me afterward, "John, you toss off these life-changing interventions into the room as if they were one-liners in a stand-up routine. Can't you see the impact you are having?" It was clear that I needed to run the risk of being seen as arrogant (another of my Shadow words) and simply acknowledge that my work *is* powerful and *does* transform lives.

Again, writing this book is a major step in that regard. (It is important to note that Bobby Knight has graduated a higher percentage of players from his basketball teams than any other active coach in NCAA Division I. His program does have validity, and he has a right to be proud of what it has done for so many young men. I am still 'going to school' with him as my own Coach in becoming more of who I am.)

⋄ 'Win at any cost to beat the competition' became *"Go all out, John, for your vision."*

Because of my Somebody Training about being humble and valuing the journey more than the destination, I have had resistance to setting goals and objectives in both my personal and business worlds. Success—and there has been a lot of it over the years—has come from people and organizations *coming to me* for what they saw, not as a result of a marketing or strategic business plan on my part. So I have been rewarded for simply responding to what 'came over the transom.'

I am convinced that this tendency to flow (or a more pejorative word, *drift*) through life—while resulting in many lives and organizations being transformed—has led me now to a situation where I must *act more purposefully.* I need to choose a course for my life and work, grab the rudder, and 'make it so.' It's time for, "Right full rudder! All ahead two-thirds!"

Like Muzak in the grocery store, your old Somebody Training tapes are still in the machine, but once you are aware of them, you can catch yourself in the (old) act and consciously substitute one of the new, still being developed skills or qualities.

Going to School with Your Shadow Character

When you squeeze out all that is wrong or evil or bad in your Shadow Character and look at what is left, you can receive powerful and spiritually enlivening insights. This is especially true when the character is one you have deeply hated.

Charlie, another Intensive participant, picked Timothy McVeigh—responsible for the terrible destruction of the Federal Building in Oklahoma City—to be his Shadow. On reflection, he saw that McVeigh:

⋄ had a clear vision,

⋄ wanted to make a large point to many people,

⋄ was resourceful,

⋄ persistent, and

⋄ believed in something so strongly that he was willing to die for it.

Charlie realized that all five of these characteristics were dramatically missing from his life and work.

Jean chose Adolf Hitler for her Shadow Character and almost cried at the suggestion that she go to school with him. When I invited her to squeeze all that was evil out of him and look at what was left, she—with a lot of help from her fellow participants—saw that Hitler was:

⋄ a powerful motivator and orator,

⋄ capable of getting large numbers of people on board with his vision, who

⋄ built an effective nation where there had been mostly chaos, and

⋄ thought big. (What could be bigger than taking over the world?)

She admitted that her life and career would benefit significantly the more she practiced putting these traits to work, ones that had been programmed out of her

Autopilot during her Somebody Training, leaving her thinking small, nervous about speaking to more than a few people, and a somewhat disorganized manager.

Judi Neal, innovative founder of the Spirit@Work Network, chose Jabba the Hutt as her Shadow Character because she saw him as sloppy, disgusting, totally self-absorbed, fat, and ugly. Not exactly the kind of person you want to take home to meet the family.

But when Judi looked at what Jabba had to teach her, she saw the following:

⋄ "He's a great delegator. He's always telling people to do things. I tend to feel like I'm responsible for doing it all. He's showing me that it would be good for me to practice asking other people to do some things for me."

⋄ "You would have to say that Jabba is stable! He has a broad base; he's hard to move off his position. He's definitely not a pushover! I need to learn when to stand my ground and not be so understanding and flexible. I think I fail to notice moments when what I need to do is stand firm and not move off my position."

⋄ "Watching him eat those grapes—or whatever it was he ate—strikes me as being sensuous, not afraid to enjoy himself. I need to nurture myself a lot more, take better care of my self, have some fun, just let it go more often—eat something decadent, like a chocolate sundae every now and then!"

You have now identified two powerful and life shaping internal realities, your Persona and your Shadow. They appear to be exact opposites. How can they co-exist, much less work together on your behalf?

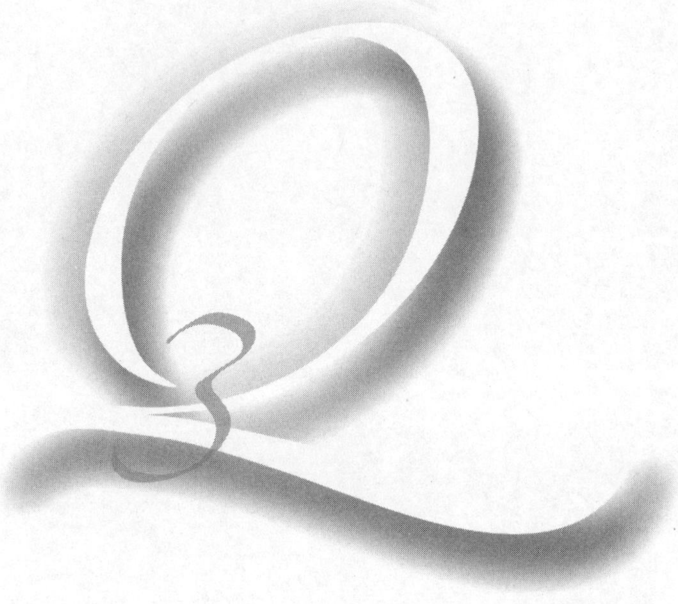

Polarity Management

B arry Johnson, a good friend and colleague, has developed a simple but deceptively profound model that shows you exactly how to work creatively with these kinds of apparent internal opposites. In his book, *Polarity Management*, Barry says, "A lot of what we consider problems to be solved can never be solved because they are actually polarities that need to be managed." Usually applied to larger organizational issues, when Barry and his wife, Dana, did the Intensive, we saw immediately that Polarity Management principles would be useful tools for discovering and bringing forth the best of the Persona and Shadow in a way that multiplies the benefits. Without this map and guidance, you could be left trying to fly on one wing— which explains why so many people seem to be going in circles, repeating old patterns and wondering why they are not going where they want to go.

An Example: Parenting

If I ask you, "How should you treat your children, with unconditional love or love with limits?" you will see immediately that as soon as you choose one, the other option not only doesn't go away, it becomes even more important. That's how you can tell when something is a true polarity, and duality exists everywhere at home and at work.

We are programmed to *compare*. We compare ourselves to others; we compare things we are thinking about buying; we compare religions and political positions. We compare everything, all the time, and sooner or later prefer one over the other, seeing one as relatively 'good' and the other as relatively 'bad.' Here is a list. Test whether you automatically prefer one over the other:

'Good'	'Bad'
Success	Failure
Lean	Fat
Rich	Poor
Free	Controlled
Making the sale	Not making the sale
Winning the argument	Losing the argument
Empowered teams	Top-down management
Quality	Cost
Change	Stability
Taking care of oneself	Taking care of others
Loving unconditionally	Loving within limits
Neat	Messy
Quiet	Loud
My Persona	My Shadow
Fast	Deliberate
Big Picture	Details

You get the idea. Virtually everything in life lives as a potential *position*, with its opposite on the other end of what is actually a continuum. We keep trying to manage our lives so we only experience things we hold as being on the 'good' side of the polarity and avoid those on the 'bad' or 'wrong' end. Life keeps reminding us that we can't live in half a world, that to be alive means living with—and discovering the benefits of—both sides of every polarity. (Remember Mark Kelso's song, *Half of Everything*, in the Introduction.)

A Time for Everything

To paraphrase the words of the biblical poet, Ecclesiastes, written over 2,500 years ago (and a more recent adaptation by Pete Seeger, recorded by The Byrds in the 1968 hit song, *Turn, Turn, Turn).*

To everything there is a season,
and a time to every purpose under heaven:
A time to be born; a time to die;
A time to plant; a time to pluck up that which is planted;
A time to kill; a time to heal;
A time to break down; a time to build up;
A time to weep; a time to laugh;
A time to mourn; a time to dance;
A time to cast away stones; a time to gather stones together;
A time to embrace; a time to refrain from embracing;
A time to gain; a time to lose;
A time to keep; a time to cast away;
A time to rend; a time to sew;
A time to keep silence; a time to speak;
A time to love; a time to hate;
A time of war; a time of peace.

We might add a more contemporary version, based on what has been developed here so far.

For everything there is a time:

A time to lead; a time to follow;

A time to express your feelings; a time to refrain from expressing;

A time to yield power; a time to wield power;

A time to talk; a time to listen;

A time for your Persona; a time for the best of your Shadow.

Our root problem in life, it seems, does not lie with the items in the negative column, like failure, fat, or loud, but rather in our *labeling the two columns in the first place. Both* columns have a crucial role to play in life. The ones we hold as bad are, at times, even essential to our development into the human being we are capable of being—if we can generate a neutral spirit of inquiry from which to explore them. 'Losing the sale' *could* become a valuable life experience. So could 'failing to get the project in on time', or 'taking care of myself.'

As my doctor, Bill Peters, tells me, "Getting sick is your body's way of trying to get your attention, John. Death is just the ultimate in feedback!" When we can suspend judgment, at least for a moment, we can see the downside of the 'positive' phenomenon and the upside of the 'negative' one. We might prefer to be rich, but the experience of being poor could be a powerful wake-up call to an even richer way of living.

Are The Maasai Poor?

Recently, on a trip to Kenya to live and work side-by-side with a Maasai community of Merrueshi, I was riding in a Land Rover with Kobole, a warrior who had become my friend. As we drove through the sprawling city of Nairobi, the driver pointed to a brown smear of cardboard and tin shacks on the side of a mountain and told us, "The estimate is that there are 500,000 people living there!" As we drove past, Kobole sat with his hand on his chin staring out the window. He turned to me and said, "I feel so sorry for those people. ... How do they know where their homes are? And they are so *poor* ..."

Later, as I recounted the moment to my colleagues Lynnea Brinkerhoff and Chris Henderson, they pointed out the amazing thing about Kobole's statement. Here sat a man who was probably *wearing* everything he owned, looking at the people in that slum and seeing *their* poverty. He was seeing a great truth, of course. Kobole had nothing, and yet had everything he needed. He was rich in the things that make for a good life:

- ⬦ He knew who he was.

- ⬦ He lived in a true community that cared about him.

- ⬦ He lived in harmony with Creator (the Maasai name for God.)

- ⬦ He lived in harmony with the earth and its plants and animals.

- ⬦ He had an extended family, a Band of Brothers who would lay down their lives for him.

- ⬦ He was genuinely happy.

It occurred to us that Kobole had what most of us only dream of having in their lives.

Good News, Bad News, Who Knows?

Many years ago, as this apocryphal story goes, there was a village in a barren land where survival was a full time job. Without horses to work the land and do heavy tasks, people would not last long. One day, a family in the village left the gate open and their old horse was able to hobble off into the wilderness. When they heard about what had happened, all the villagers came rushing to the family's place, saying, "What a terrible thing! Now what will you do?!" The family had a grandmother, a wise old crone, who looked at the grieving neighbors and said, "Good news, bad news, who knows?"

The villagers shook their heads and wandered back to their homes muttering about how the old woman had lost her marbles (or whatever it was people back then would have muttered).

Several days later, however, the old horse came trotting over the hill—with three wild horses in tow! The news spread rapidly and soon all the villagers were again standing around the family's gate saying things like, "How did you know it was going to be good news? Isn't this wonderful? Now you have *four* horses; you're the richest family in our village!" To which the crone responded, "Good news, bad news, who knows?"

Again the villagers returned to their homes grumbling at the perverse attitude of the old woman.

The next day, as the family's teenage son was out trying to break one of the wild horses, he was thrown and broke his hip in several places, crippling him for life. As word got around, the villagers came trooping around again, saying, "You were right, old woman! It was a tragedy that you got those horses. Now your grandson has been crippled for life. Awful, just awful." Again the old woman said, "Good news, bad news, who knows?"

By this time the villagers were getting used to her strange response, but it didn't stop them from wondering again whether she was really 'all there.'

Some time later a local warlord came through the village dragooning every able-bodied young man to go and fight in a battle from which few would return. He took every single young man in the village ... except for the grandson with the broken hip. At this the villagers swarmed back, shouting, "You were right! It was a good thing that your grandson broke his hip! At least now you have him around to help. What a wonderful thing!" Again, the wise old crone said, "Good news, bad news, who knows?"

Conclusions: *What Stops Us From Learning*

When does this story end? Right. It *never* ends. We are inclined, as humans, to decide immediately whether some event is good news or bad news, long before we have the perspective that comes with hindsight. The wise old crone had something we all need to develop: a way of seeing or 'holding' events in a kind of inquiry or neutral mode long enough for both the upside and the downside of the inherent polarity to manifest.

You might wonder what is wrong with the built-in penchant for making instant judgments. You do it all the time. Isn't it a crucial skill? Yes, but the instant you come to a conclusion about something—or someone—*learning stops*. You become unable to see anything different from your judgment. In fact, the stronger your emotional reaction, the more distorted your perception. Falling in love with someone is just as much about this phenomenon as having an instant dislike for them. As soon as we make the judgment—good news or bad news—we lose everything else about that person or situation that doesn't fit our assessment.

As you saw in working with your Shadow Character, there is a way to take even the worst experience of your life and find the upside, and vice versa. When you can generate an open spirit of inquiry regarding what happens to you, every experience becomes an opportunity for growth and development—and maximum contribution to others and to life.

What Would Change From Your Past?

Think of an experience that occurred earlier in your life—maybe one at work—which, at the time, you would just as soon have avoided. Perhaps it was a divorce, or a bankruptcy, or getting fired, something 'bad.' Now, temporarily suspend the judgment you have about that moment, with its accompanying anger or pain or shame, and look closely at it as a potentially life-enhancing event. How has that experience contributed positively to your becoming who you are today? What is the upside or hidden benefit in that 'negative' moment?

If Pop Had Stopped Drinking

If my father had stopped drinking when I was nine or ten years old, I would have been the happiest kid in the world, for myself, for Mom, but mostly for Pop. If that huge, life dominating, self esteem eroding problem had gone away back then, ... what joy, what relief. And, most likely, I would not be in this line of work writing this book for you. Can you see that it was my failure to transform my Pop's life that has moved me to transform every life I can get my hands on? That's one kind of good news coming out of the bad news of the alcoholic classroom I called home for seventeen years.

There's another beneficial lesson in growing up in Pop's alcoholic world. Anyone who has lived in a relationship with someone addicted to drugs or alcohol knows what it takes to survive. The skills and attributes that were sharpened on the whetstone of that frightening childhood experience have stood me in good stead in my work ever since. For instance, I learned how to read between the lines of what people were saying in order to hear what they really meant—a great asset as a therapist, consultant, and leadership development coach. I would get up from breakfast, get on my bike and, on the way to school, be thinking, "It's going to be rough tonight ..."

It was a survival skill to sense when a storm was coming so I could batten down the hatches and prepare for heavy weather—something which enables me today to discern what people are feeling, sometimes even before they know it themselves. In the absence of a lot of positive reinforcement or emotional support around the house, I developed the capacity to fend for myself, to be my own source of 'juice' for life.

All of that—my desire to be a force for positive change in people's lives and the skills required to be effective in this kind of deep work—came *directly* out of my family being *exactly* the way it was. Good news, bad news, who knows? As a young boy whose gifts and direction in life were being hammered out daily on that family anvil, I was not able to see and embrace the polarities present. That didn't happen until later. Much later.

Managing The Persona-Shadow Polarity

To assist in the process of seeing the potential upside of a Shadow characteristic you have pushed aside or resisted—as well as seeing the potential downside of a habitual alternative with which you are enamored—Barry Johnson developed the Polarity Map. This visually shows how two apparent opposites can be understood as the poles of a continuum that needs to be managed, rather than a war with a winner and a loser. As Barry points out, we humans tend to see the world in terms of opposites and then prefer one over the other. Hot and cold, good and bad, right and wrong, up and down, success and failure. We are hard-wired to choose one pole or position over another in virtually every aspect of life and work.

A whole array of difficult situations and opportunities faces you all day every day. Many of these contain polarities to be managed, not problems to be solved. Polarities are both unavoidable and unsolvable. Because polarities have been in our lives since birth, all of us have learned through experience and intuition to manage many of them fairly well. We know how to both plan *and* take action. We need to be clear *and* flexible. We encourage individual initiative *and* team synergy. We know how to rest *and* work. Much of the time, though, most people end up *getting positional* and relying on only one side of the polarity. We create an *either-or* situation, where actually there exists a *both-and*.

⋄ Should we reward teams *or* individual performers?

⋄ Should I attend to my needs *or* my family's needs?

⋄ Should we have top-down decision-making *or* bottom-up decision-making?

⋄ Is it to be change *or* stability?

⋄ Do I pursue career development *or* focus on where I am right now?

You know you're in a polarity to be managed when one position 'wins' over the other, but *the other pole or option not only does not go away but becomes even more important.* For instance, when you decide to make a change, the need for stability is still present. Or vice versa. That's because a polarity represents two ongoing, interdependent variables that actually need each other.

Let's say that two parents, Joe and Sue, are in an argument about how to raise the kids, and the two are locked into their opposite polar positions. Joe's position is called 'unconditional love' and Sue's is called 'setting boundaries.' Let's say further that each of them feels so strongly about their position that they know they are right, they want to win, and want the other to lose—and see how wrong they are. Let's say Joe wins the argument and Sue submits to his victory, resulting in a parental style based on nothing but unconditional love. What happens to the kids? What happens to the need for them to discover and come to grips with boundaries?

Can you see that Sue's position really doesn't go away just because she lost the argument? In fact, it becomes even more important. So, the answer to the question, "Should we raise our kids with unconditional love or set boundaries?" is "Yes." If either polar position wins, the kids ultimately lose.

Here's another analogy: When lumberjacks are using a two-person cross buck saw, the cut comes on the draw. For Joe to get his maximum cut, Sue must maintain a certain amount of tension on the saw, and vice versa. Each must let the other person get their cut, but pull back just a little, otherwise the other person won't be able to cut at all. If one of the people and their position 'loses' or is not there, the 'winner' who is trying to cut will at best get a single cut, or more likely, the saw will wobble and freeze up.

The application to my work that I saw in Barry's model is this: Polarities not only exist between people or between points of view in organizations, but *inside individuals* as well. The Persona/Shadow work you explored earlier should now be starting to come together and make some sense. Can you see how they represent a Polarity to be managed?

The Natural Polarity Of Breathing

Barry uses the example of breathing to show how natural polarities occur in life.

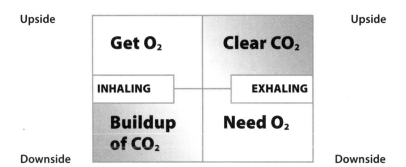

Inhaling and Exhaling are both essential for life. Fortunately for us, however, breathing was not left up to our thinking brain. If we had to think about breathing, we'd all be dead, not because we would forget to breathe—although that may be a possibility—but because if our minds were involved at all, we would develop a preference for one pole! "I'm an Inhaler, what are you?" We would be trying to live by experiencing only our preferred position, and within a few minutes we'd be dead.

Don't overlook these fundamental principles:

⋄ Inhaling not only has an upside—getting oxygen—but also a downside—the build-up of carbon dioxide.

⋄ You cannot get the upside—oxygen—without having the parallel experience of the build-up of CO_2. This is important. You get oxygen, you get CO_2. They come together.

⋄ The same goes, in reverse, for exhaling. You clear CO_2; you need oxygen.

⋄ The body doesn't prefer one over the other; that's why we're still alive. It has sensing mechanisms throughout the body—in every cell, actually—that monitor and trigger when it is time to move to the other position.

⋄ As long as we remain healthy, this process has become an effortless and conflict-free experience. We don't get nervous, when we are in the exhaling phase, worrying about getting back to inhaling.

Application

If this physical example seems simplistic, let's look at the Persona and Shadow as polarities begging to be understood and integrated. Here's what my own internal Polarity Map looks like:

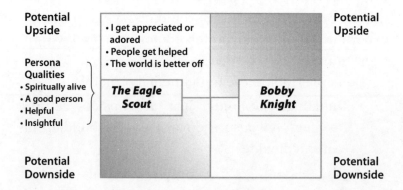

As you can see, the Upside of being The Eagle Scout includes benefits to myself, to other people and to the world in general; but if I had to walk around all day being an Eagle Scout—and that was all I had available to me—the Downsides would eventually begin to manifest:

⬦ exhaustion from having to help or save everyone else all the time.

⬦ a subtle kind of disempowering of those around me who might also have the necessary skills and desire to help.

⬦ missing what is going just fine around me—always seeing what needs help.

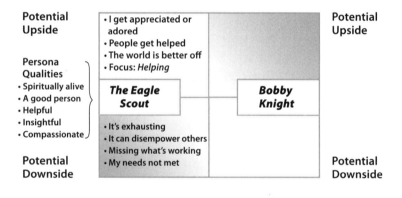

When the Persona's Downside begins to show up, the mind thinks, "Maybe I should do something different; this isn't really working. Maybe I should try something from 'the other side, over there' (a little more like Bobby Knight)." Instantly the Autopilot alarm goes off, *Bong, Bong, Bong, Dive, Dive, Dive.* "For Pete's sake, John, don't even *think* about going over to the Bobby Knight way of being! You *know* what's over there!" Of course, all the mind's attention is focused on the Downside of the opposite pole. "If you go over there, John, you'll get dumped, reviled, replaced, people will get hurt and you'll make a lot of people angry. Just try harder to make the Eagle Scout thing work."

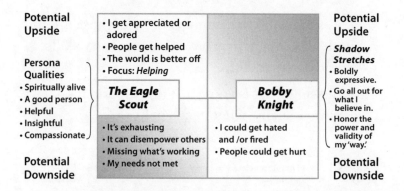

So we go back to work, pumping up our Persona even more, hoping for a breakthrough, which rarely comes. What we desperately need is something from our Shadow—the other pole of our polarity, but our Autopilot, with its default programming, kicks in and prevents us from even putting our toe in that water. In the process, we lose access to what our soul is crying for, the Upside of the Shadow. It takes some work, but when you see these benefits, the insight brings relief and joy.

Revealing The Upside Of The Shadow

Look again at the Stretches exercise on Page 157. Write your top three or four in the space beside your Shadow character on the map:

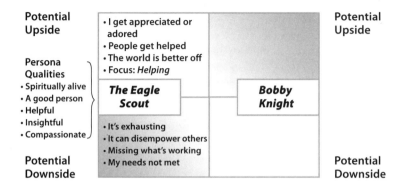

Putting It All Together

Now think about this: if you had access to *these* qualities and attributes, what might then become possible? How might you, others, and life benefit?

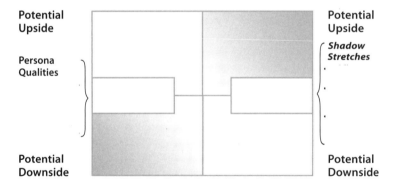

Whether you fill this in silently or in fact, this is worth your contemplation.

Chapter Thirteen

The Inner Polarity

It ought to be abundantly clear at this point that we have inside ourselves an internal polarity that begs to be managed, or at least acknowledged: the Persona and the Shadow. The 'good stuff' and the 'I never want to be like *that* stuff.' When you are unaware of these two characters battling away inside, you end up at the effect of the war.

What Bobby Knight Has To Teach Me

As I develop the courage to explore these Stretches from the pole beside my Bobby Knight character—who doesn't stop himself out of concern for how others might react—new possibilities open up as transformation begins to happen:

⬥ Being boldly expressive. The more I express my true feelings sooner and trust other people to handle what comes next, the more effective—

and expressed—I am. As the Eagle Scout, my Somebody Training wants me to be self-contained to make sure I can be helpful to others, at my own expense if necessary. Over time, if I do not have permission to rest and respond to my own needs, my capacity and motivation to help others drops off sharply. I don't have to throw chairs or hit people simply to let my emotions out—even a little—every now and then.

The Afghanistan Sermon

I remember the Sunday that we went into Afghanistan in response to the attacks of 9/11. As a veteran, I had been walking a tight line between my desire for revenge against those who had perpetrated such heartless acts on thousands of innocent civilians, and my heartfelt compassion for the people of Afghanistan, who were about to get clobbered by America's military might. The congregation where I preached occasionally was also split, being the worshipping community for people from the military as well as the pacifist worlds. I heard about the attack just after the 8:30am worship service. I was so torn about our unfolding war that I scrapped my existing sermon and, at the 10:45am service, I told the congregation, "There is no sermon this morning. There's just what is going on inside of me right now." And I proceeded to describe my polarized emotions.

On the one hand, I said I wanted to bomb bin Laden back to where he came from, to show others like him that they couldn't get away with terrorism, and that even as a 61-year-old, if the US Navy called me up for some kind of hazardous duty in that effort, I would go and fight. On the other hand, I said I wanted America to become a force for peace in the world, and that at the same time we were doing what had to be done in punishing the bad guys, we also needed to look to our own role in creating and maintaining a world where this kind of violence seemed the only solution to many oppressed people.

After church, as I stood at the door to greet people, I held my breath, concerned about the upset I might have caused by being so blunt about my feelings. (The Eagle Scout and his Autopilot/Con at work again.) I was blown away by the response. "Thanks, John, for your honesty." "You never talk about your personal positions on things, John, and now I feel like I know you better." And this one, which truly surprised me, coming from a Vietnam-era Marine Colonel, "I don't always agree with what you have to say, John—sometimes you seem too liberal for my taste—but I appreciate hearing where you stand on this. Now I think I can trust you even more."

The Lesson Learned: a little of my Bobby Knight character's willingness to express boldly how he feels every now and then can be *exactly* what is called for.

⬦ Going all out for what I believe in, rather than stopping myself for fear of being seen as arrogant, opens doors to things getting accomplished that might not occur if I always worry about what people might think. Being nice all the time is not enough; it certainly isn't whole or complete. Imagine my being in a situation where I need to be a tough directive leader, and there I am, trying to 'nice' my way through it. Yuk!

The Tough Leader

As the polarity map makes clear, we have the Shadow 'in there' somewhere, yearning to be allowed to find expression in our lives. I have the tough leader in me, for sure.

When I decided that I would run my first marathon some years ago, I told my friends and neighbors, thus painting myself into a corner and having to do what I said I would do. I make my living mostly with words. You can't *talk* your way around twenty-six miles, or imagine your way there; you have to *do* it. That requires going all out for what is important, every day for six months of training.

This kind of experience has helped identify the Spiritual Warrior who lives in me—and whose energy, strength and toughness is a welcome adjunct to the kind, compassionate healer who lives right beside him in my soul.

⬦ Having the courage to honor my own work and way of being. I have been so concerned about being seen as a 'true believer' who doesn't respect other paths to truth that I have been reluctant to acknowledge my role in creating this powerful approach to personal transformation. It has been hard for me to act as if what I do is life changing, or to promote my work with implied promises of breakthrough; but this book is a breakthrough in that regard. *This Five Questions process does in fact transform lives.*

What's Been Running You?

So, what's been running you at home and at work? Your Autopilot, or Con, which is dedicated to making sure you always stay safe and look good. It accomplishes this feat by manipulating you, those around you, and even life itself. You now have the ingredients necessary to see what has been running you, your unconscious formula for success. By seeing it, then naming it, even speaking it out loud, its power is reduced, and it no longer 'has you' and you can expand your life into what calls you. Try yours on, using this format:

Your Con/Default Formula for Success

Hello, I am _____, but I have been presenting myself to you as _____, who is _____, _____, and _____, and working hard to keep you from seeing me as _____, who is _____, _____, and _____, so you will _____ me and not _____ me.

This has been my Con up until now. I hereby honor its original noble intention, I release its control over my life, and I open myself to living the greater truth of who I am.

Here's my own Con, my default Formula for Success:

> Hello, I'm <u>John</u>, but I've been presenting myself to you as <u>the Eagle Scout</u>, who is <u>brave, insightful, clever, and transformational,</u> and working hard to keep you from seeing me as <u>Bobby Knight</u>, who is <u>emotionally out of control, mean, and arrogant,</u> so you will <u>adore and respect me (then I know I matter),</u> and not <u>dump, replace, or revile me (then I would know I don't matter).</u>
>
> *This has been my Con up until now. I hereby honor its original noble intention, I release its reign over my life, and open myself to living fully the truth of who I am.*

When I saw the truth of this, I admitted to myself that, when I was unconscious and on Autopilot, I was going around trying to *matter,* to impress people with how clever and transformational I was so they would adore me. When I saw *that,* it was so powerful an insight—and so upsetting—I knew I had to get beyond this 'game' to what *else* my life might be about. Something larger, something more worthy of who I am. I knew I had to discover—or actually re-discover—to fully explore the fourth of the FIVE QUESTIONS: WHAT CALLS ME?

Question 4: What calls me?

Chapter Fourteen

Living A Purpose Worthy of Who You Are

Having taken on Question 3: WHAT RUNS ME? perhaps you can now see how you have been living your life guided by an Autopilot, employing a (mostly) unconscious Con designed to get regular 'hits' of what your Somebody Training said you needed (your Addiction), and avoid any hint of what that training told you would be deadly (your Terror). It all adds up to a life based on a strategy developed a l-o-n-g time ago intended to keep you safe and looking good.

The question posed next is: If *that* is not what you are on the planet for, then *why are you here*? When you get beyond, or beneath, all that Automatic Living programmed into you, what are you putting yourself—the wonderful attributes from your Persona and the powerful Stretches in your Shadow—in the service of?

In short, WHAT CALLS YOU?

The Call From Outside

The more obvious response to this question has to do with what calls you from *outside*, from the world. In fact, the concept of being 'called' is at the root of our word 'vocation' (from the Latin, *vocare*—to call or speak), and is usually associated with people in religious roles. In the past, those who heard and responded to 'the call' were known as 'ecclesiastical' (from the Greek, *ekleseia*—the called out ones). Like today's volunteer fire fighters, when the divine siren went off, they were the ones who heard it and responded. Looked at in this vein, the question would be: *What calls to you from the world? What is a need that exists 'out there' that grabs you and won't let you go?* We will return to this call from outside a little later in this chapter.

Frederick Beutner's words make a perfect transition here: *The place Life calls you to is the place where your deep gladness and the world's deep hunger meet.*

Let's first explore "your deep gladness," or what calls you from inside.

The Call From Inside

As important as the world's needs are, taking on Question 4 is not initially about what calls you from *outside*, or about what job or task should you should set yourself to. Questions like, "What would be the best place for me to 'aim' myself and my gifts?" or "Should I be doing what I am doing now?" are crucial to ask yourself, but they come later.

Other questions need to come first:

⋄   What inside me calls out to be expressed into the world?

⋄   What in me simply must be manifest in whatever work I do?

⋄   What is my soul here to learn and to contribute?

Before you decide what *job* you should take on out there in the world, you must take on the *inner work* of reconnecting with your own soul and its essence. The word 'job', by the way, comes from the Old English word *gobbe*, referring to how laborers got paid back then—by the *lump* of whatever they were hauling or shoveling. 'Work' on the other hand, comes from the Greek word *erg*, which, if I remember my high school physics, is a measure of how much force it takes to move one gram one centimeter. Work is energy with a vector. You could say *work is purposeful energy being exerted in a specific direction.*

If you only search for the job 'out there' and fail to base it on the work that is most truly about you 'in here', no matter how important the external task you take on, eventually you—and that task—will founder. What you DO on the outside must be connected deeply and directly with who you ARE on the inside.

The rest of nature understands this. An acorn would never try to become a pine tree; it has to become an oak tree. It must grow into what it is designed or intended to be. I am not implying, as some would argue, that there is a divine plan that you have to fit into. If that were the case, then this whole book and the notion of doing any inner work would be rendered useless. Put the book down and simply keep doing what you're doing—and hope the plan is in place. That kind of fatalism is not what this is about.

What Is Your Charism?

What I am suggesting is that each of us has inside a tendency or urge to manifest something out there in the world that is connected with who and what is deep within us. Throughout history that urge has been the focus of attention for profound thinkers and spiritual teachers, and has been called the *charism* (pronounced care-ism). You know that word. We say it about special people we see as charismatic. Originally, for the Greeks who named it, a charism was simply a *gift*, seen as a divinely proffered ability to know or do things. The truth is that we are all gifted, each in our own way. No one is left out. The question isn't: *Am I gifted or not?* but rather: *What are those gifts that make me who I am?*

Artists understand this charism principle. Throughout history they have been the ones among us who realize their charism, and allow it to express itself in their work. They will tell you, in fact, that they feel *compelled* to express that creative urge or knowing, turning it into something that can be seen or heard in the physical world.

If you look back over the various jobs you have had, you may be able to see the footprint of your charisms, your core gifts, your essence, or soul's qualities. Perhaps you can see the inner theme that has woven itself through what you have been doing on the outside all along.

A *Personal Example*
In my life, I have had many different jobs, shown here in chronological order, starting with the first work I had in my teens:

- ❖ YMCA camp counselor/Waterfront and Program Director
- ❖ amateur/professional magician, mostly birthdays and business clubs like Rotary and Kiwanis
- ❖ AAU Swim Team coach
- ❖ Combat Officer, USS *Eaton* (DD-510), US Navy
- ❖ Lutheran minister/university chaplain/ counselor and family therapist
- ❖ core faculty member of a graduate program in applied behavioral science
- ❖ leadership and executive development coach
- ❖ organizational change and conflict consultant, seminar leader, and author

Can you see any themes here? On the surface, these eight jobs appear to be quite different and unrelated, but when I look into them more closely, I see a *pattern*. I can get a sense of my *charism* at work in each of them. It took a wake up call of major proportions to make it clear, however.

An *Unavoidable Message*:   *In case you missed it, John*
One afternoon, when I was about to finish my four years of service in the Navy and was unsure of what came next, I remember going off watch and heading

to my stateroom in the After Officers' Quarters on the ship. Gently lulled by the rolling of the sea, which was as smooth as glass that day, I sat down alone at my little pull-down desk, took out a clean pad of yellow, lined paper, and began to think about what I ought to do with my life after my tour of duty was up. On one side of the paper I made a list of all the things I could think of that I *might like* to do. As I recall, I wrote down things like:

- ⋄ *Boy Scout executive* (As an Eagle Scout, Order of the Arrow, and Senior Patrol Leader of my Troop, this one made some sense.)

- ⋄ *YMCA youth worker or camp director* (I had been a Counselor, Assistant Program Director, and Waterfront Director for many summers at Camp Richmond.)

- ⋄ *social worker* (An aunt, Harriet Anne, had been one in Pennsylvania and it sounded like I could do some good in that role.)

- ⋄ *doctor* (A cousin was a surgeon, and the practice of medicine intrigued me.)

- ⋄ *teacher* (Homer Bast, my close friend and Roanoke College Faculty Advisor, had been an inspiration to me, and I often pictured myself standing in front of a class, teaching history.)

- ⋄ *minister* (With five generations out of six in the gene pool on my father's side serving as Lutheran Ministers, this one had to be in there.)

- ⋄ *insurance* (Jim Heslep, my Scout Leader, had invited me to join him in his practice with Traveler's when I got out of the Navy.)

Then I made a list down the other side of the paper (I can't believe I was such a Virgo about this) of things I would *never do*, like:

⋄ *CPA or bookkeeper* (It was a Herculean effort just to balance my checkbook.)

⋄ *salesman, e.g.* real estate, automobiles, 'things'

⋄ *career US Naval Officer* (My Captain, Pehr Pehrsson, had urged me to stay in, but it just didn't feel 'right' to me.)

⋄ any role that required me to do the same thing over and over every day, or

⋄ any job that was focused on making money

I stared at that piece of paper for a long time and nothing came to me. I remember feeling discouraged and a little lost. After about an hour of internal wrestling, a question formed, not so much in my mind as in my heart, my gut. In retrospect, it now appears to have been a kind of prayer: *What should I do with my life?*

What happened next can only be described as a moment of divine inspiration, what a Zen or yoga master would call an enlightenment experience, or a theophany, to use biblical language.

A voice came to me, as clear as a bell, "*John. ... (long pause) Be with people at the level of their deepest need.*"

I remember asking reflexively in US Navy Air Controller lingo, "*Say again, over.*"

The voice obliged, "*John, be with people at the level of their deepest need.*"

Wishing the voice could have been a little more specific, I immediately realized that what I got was all

I was going to get—there weren't going to be any more details. The rest was up to me to figure out. I wrote it down as fast as I could, lest I forget it.

What that voice did was tell me—or remind me—what my charism was. What the 'acorn' inside was all actually about. It didn't say anything about the oak tree—the *result* of my charism, the outside manifestation, the *job*; it just put me in touch with the acorn, the *inner essence*, my *work*. That is, apparently, enough. When I look back at each of the *jobs* I have had in my life, that acorn of inner *work* has permeated the way I approached the outer work. In each of them, I was intending to be of service to the people around me. It wouldn't matter what job came down the road, what I brought to it—the John J. Scherer IV acorn or charism would be the same: Be with people at the level of their deepest need.

Even as a Combat Officer on a US Navy destroyer! One afternoon the ship's Executive Officer, LCDR Bob Clark, stopped me in passing on the starboard side of the main deck and, smiling, asked me, "Mr. Scherer, what are you running here, a ship of war or a psychiatric clinic?" I remember waggling the fingers of my extended right hand and saying, "Well, XO, it depends on when you ask." Even there, in that hard environment where life was literally on the line every day, someone *else* had picked up my soul's theme, my acorn, my charism, my *work*.

A *Polaroid Moment*

Many years later, while in the first day of a two-day Leadership Development training session for a group of mid-level managers from Polaroid, one of the participants stopped me, almost in midsentence.

"John, what are you *really* doing here with us? I mean, all you consultants have the same little diagrams and buzz words; we hear them over and over; but there's something *different* about this stuff you're doing, and I just can't put my finger on it. What's going on here?"

I noticed other heads nodding in agreement as he spoke. So, like a good consultant (when in doubt, gather data), I asked people to say what was going on for them.

"Man, oh man. I feel like I'm at church camp!" one participant said. There was laughter around the room. "No!" he went on, "I mean I haven't felt this alive and good and hopeful about my life in a l-o-n-g time. Not since church camp!"

"Well, I concur," a woman chimed in. "This feels like a spiritual development seminar to me. Let's GO! I'm loving it!"

"Okay, I'll keep this feedback going," another manager chimed in. " You're showing us a bunch of really useful and interesting stuff, John, but there is some kind of deeper dimension to what is happening here—more than just typical leadership models and theories. You seem to be touching us at another, I'll call it spiritual, level."

Now you have to understand that I had never used the word 'spiritual' or even had that notion anywhere in my intention for this seminar. I had been presenting straightforward leadership and management concepts and models, like the Life

Cycle of Organizations, Three Kinds of Change, Dealing with Resistance, and The Waterline. Stuff like that. Not an overtly spiritual notion in any of it! Puzzled, but intrigued, I thanked them and picked up my magic marker to continue.

"Wait a minute, John!" the first guy stopped me. "You haven't answered my question: What *are* you doing here with us?"

Something 'went deep' in me, and I chose not to rattle off some glib, clever retort—which I was certainly capable of. Instead, I chose to drop into that inner place where I go when meditating, and see what came. Internally, I told myself that I would say—without editing—whatever rose to the surface of my mind.

"Let me think about that for a moment," I recall saying and I just stood still in front of them, waiting for what would come. When it came a few seconds later, I spoke it into the room, feeling amazed and excited by what it had turned out to be:

"I am here to love you and be a channel for the truth."

Wow! It hit me like a ton of bricks. It must have hit everyone else, too, because the room got *v-e-r-y* still. You could have heard a pin drop. No one moved. There was a kind of crackling clearness in the air, like after a rainstorm when there has been lightning. Still no one moved. I didn't know what to do. The stillness went on for quite a while. I didn't want to break the moment and disrupt whatever was moving in us by saying anything, so I simply stood quietly—and reverently—in the powerful experience enveloping us.

After what seemed like forever, I said quietly, "Perhaps we should take a short break." (I didn't know what else to do.)

Still no one moved. Then, very slowly, almost reluctantly, people began to quietly get up and walk out to the hall. Even during the break, while people got juice or coffee, there was little or no speaking. One manager came up to me and whispered, "John, what in the world was *that*?" I didn't know what to say. So I shrugged and said, "I don't know, but it was something, wasn't it?"

In retrospect, I would call that moment another theophany, an experience of divine energy breaking through the hold of the mind to touch someone with a provocative truth, or knowing.

Chapter Fifteen

Discovering Your Special Gifts

You, too, have had such moments, whether or not you have been aware of them. It happens in a less dramatic way every time your charism is at work, when your soul's essence is being expressed into life. It happens when you are BEING yourself, all out, and not just DOING what your programming tells you to do.

What Calls You: *Finding Your Charism*

People we call charismatic are simply those whose soul or essence or charism or *work* is being expressed in the *job* they are doing. So, since you have been gifted with charism, too, you—and everyone else—are potentially charismatic. All you need to do is discover what your charism is and begin allowing it to express itself in your work. Here are a few things to think about that will help you get started:

⋄ What are the bone deep talents, gifts, tendencies and/or skills in you that 'make your heart sing' when you do them?

⋄ What are you really good at that you never had to learn—you just always seem to have had the ability?

⋄ What would you almost do for nothing because it brought you so much joy?

⋄ What would be a purpose worthy of who you are?

The Breakthrough Moment

This last question is one that transformed my life—and started me on the path that led to the FIVE QUESTIONS— and eventually to this book.

In 1982, the organization effectiveness survey business I had started with two colleagues went belly up. One partner went Chapter 7 and declared personal bankruptcy, and the other partner essentially bailed out. Both their choices were actually fine with me, but it meant that I was left holding a bag containing about $175,000 in unpaid bills and other obligations, mostly to good friends and trusting family members who had invested in our venture. Based on advice from my business and financial advisors and the encouragement of my wife, as well as my own commitment to get this 'money karma' cleaned up once and for all, I decided to stick it out and dig my way out of debt.

To help with this embarrassing and, for me, shameful situation, I called in a favor from a colleague, Dixon de Leña, at that time a Seattle based breakthrough consultant. He flew over to Spokane where I was living, and during a day of intense personal and spiritual probing, asked me, "John, what's been *driving* you? What has been your reason for living, your no kidding purpose?" Something in the way he asked me led me to look inside before answering.

Looking back, I realize that instead of having my *mind* respond with something that would put a positive spin on the situation, thus salvaging some vestige of self-protection, I asked my *soul* for the truth, no matter how embarrassing, and for the courage to put it out there and let the chips fall where they may. After what seemed like an eternity, the truth came to me:

"My reason for living recently? What's been driving me? No kidding? I'm here to get out of debt and make it through the next quarter." I blurted, feeling both surprised and relieved at the answer. In fact, as I spoke that authentic truth to Dixon, a clear sense of calm and deep peace came over me. One of Jesus' sayings came to mind. "You will know the truth, and the truth will set you free." This truth sure did. I felt free—not from the debt, which still had to be repaid—but free from the fear of failure and shame that had been my constant companion for a long time.

"Thanks, John, for your honesty." Then Dixon asked me the question that started changing my life. *"Is that a purpose worthy of who you are?* Are you on this planet to get out of debt and make it through the next quarter? Or could there be more to your being here than that?"

Dixon's question, like all life transforming questions, stunned me to such an extent that I didn't know what to say. After a moment, he stepped into the silence: "What about this phrase in your letterhead, John, *transforming the world at work*? Could *that* be what you are up to underneath all that concern about debt and your reputation?"

"Nahh," I said, "that's just a marketing phrase I made up in the shower one day."

"Okay," Dixon smiled. "When you figure out what you are truly up to, call me and we'll go forward from there."

He left for Seattle, leaving me in a grateful but confused state of inquiry. As you will see, this is precisely the state that heralds personal transformation. Several months went by as I chewed on his question. What *was* a purpose worthy of who I was? It took three months of thinking, musing, internal thrashing, and living in the question. When the deeper truth emerged, it was another surprise. As is often the case, the answer was sitting right in front of me. I called Dixon.

"Hey, Dix, this is John. I think I've got it!"

"Okay, I'll bite." I could hear the smile in his voice. "What are you really up to underneath all the stuff about survival and reputation?"

"What I'm really up to is *transforming the world at work*. Turns out that phrase was coming from a more profound place than I realized. Whenever I think about it, my soul hums like a guitar string."

"Congratulations, John! You have finally figured out what anyone who has known you for five minutes can see immediately! You may have thought you were all about getting out of debt and making it through the next quarter, but those of us who know you knew better. Now let's begin to build that new enterprise you have been wanting to create. But it has to be built not on fear and façade but on truth."

It Is Too Light A Thing That You Do.'

About the same time as my conversation with Dixon, I was preparing for a sermon at St. Mark's Lutheran Church in Spokane where I was invited to speak from time to time. In our tradition, we begin sermon preparation with three stories from the Bible that are assigned for that Sunday. One of them that week turned out to be from the book of Isaiah, who, in this particular segment, was busy being a messenger to the people of Judah but not getting a very positive reception. He was feeling low (today we would probably say he was depressed), and complained to God. The answer that came to Isaiah nailed me to the wall:

> *It is too light a thing that you do, Isaiah,*
> *just going to the tribes of Jacob to restore the*
> *survivors of Israel. I want you to be a light to all*
> *the nations, so that my healing love will reach to*
> *the ends of the earth. (translation mine)*
> –Isaiah 49:6

The message: "Isaiah, I'm sorry you're so depressed because people have not been responding like you want, but what you have been up to—just bringing my love to *your* people—is not 'weighty' enough. You need to expand and deepen your concept of what you are about. I want you to start reaching out to *everyone on earth*." I get this translation because in the original language, the word 'light' used here is the opposite of the word *kavod,* which means 'weight' or 'heavy' or 'impact.' Isaiah is being chastised for playing too small, playing it safe, doing what contains the least risk, or is the most familiar. *He is not having the impact he yearns for because he is not being who he is capable of being.*

As usual, at that point I asked myself, "What is the lesson for *you* in this story?" The answer came immediately: "John, it is too light a thing you are doing. This does not mean you need to become an overextended, stressed-out, Type A, do-gooder. It *does* mean you need to step back and take a hard look at what you have been up to in your life and see whether it is big enough, impactful enough. Look to see whether where you are aiming all your gifts is worthy of who you are. What are you putting those talents and gifts in the service of? You have been 'playing too small.'"

Ouch. When I truly let this in, it meant that I needed to stop thinking it was enough to put my gifts to work getting people to sign up for my seminars, or to generate enough consulting projects each month to make payroll. I could imagine a divine voice saying, "No! Those are just table stakes! You are not here to fill seminars and make payroll! You are here to contribute to the transformation of the world at work, and the unleashing of the human spirit. Get after *that*, John Scherer! That's far 'heavier' for you and a far more meaningful reason to be alive."

Trimming The Load

The first year after my near-bankruptcy and Dixon's coaching, our taxable income was $24,000, with around $9,000 going to Minneapolis for child-support and $12,000 for the mortgage. We jettisoned everything but the barest essentials. We cancelled the cable TV, the newspaper, all our magazines. We sold a car and most of the living room furniture. We even sold some of my old magic tricks to a collector. Then we hunkered down with our infant son, Asa, and I set out to create a new consulting firm, with a mission of *transforming the world at work.*

Thanks to the generosity of several well-established friends and colleagues in the field, Ron Lippitt, Herb Shepard, and Jack Sherwood, consulting and speaking projects started to come in. Good work, you could say, the kind that meant transforming the world at work. The next year our income doubled, then doubled again the next year, and again the next, and so on until the growing little firm was generating close to $800,000 a year.

That's not the point, though! In spite of what some motivational speakers and TV evangelists want us to believe, it doesn't always happen that way. Your income doesn't always go up when you wake up and step into what calls you. There have been several lean years since then, too.

The reward for waking up and stepping into what calls you is—ready?—waking up and stepping into what calls you. That's the payoff. What could be more meaningful than doing work that makes your heart sing, putting into action that which you ARE. Of course, it's risky and requires an act of faith. The fears are natural and predictable: *What if no one is interested in what I am doing with this insight? How will I/we eat?*

Consider the alternative: the Con, the Adaptive Routine—going around all day trying to be something you think will 'sell' and getting little hits of what you are addicted to. That's what most people are doing. It works—kind of. On the surface. For a while. Until the rot sets in. Then 'something happens.' Maybe a heart attack, or a merger that lays you off, or a family crisis, or you get depressed, and you are forced to stop and take stock. When that happens, you have to examine carefully the fundamental 'game' you have been playing. If you look closely, here's what it probably looks like. It's the default strategy I call the Deferred Life Plan:

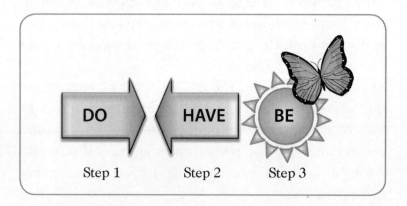

You probably know The Deferred Life Plan well, but let me graphically lay it out for you. It starts at the left and runs like this:

⋄ You are to DO whatever you have to do, sacrifice your health, your family, your sanity, your friendships, and put it all at risk so that one day you can

⋄ HAVE what you need to have. When you have enough of whatever that is (money, fame, success, Prince/Princess Charming), you can *then* get to

⋄ BE whatever it is that you are after in life (happy, secure, at peace, fulfilled).

You can see why I call this the *Deferred* Life Plan. The rules of the game dictate that you don't get to truly live until later on, but like some life insurance policies, you have to die—or almost die—to win. You have to postpone—and earn—that state you are yearning for: probably something like peace of mind, security, or deep fulfillment. One day, in the future, when you have accumulated enough _____ (fill in the blank), *then* you can allow yourself to relax and live.

Since so many people around the world are applying this approach, it must be a *very* successful way to live. In fact, we have found only one small problem with it. It doesn't work. Sorry. It would be so cool if it did. Then, all we would have to do is work hard, accumulate stuff, and *shazzam*, we'd be 'there.' It works for a moment or two, like just after you make the sale, or get the promotion, or find Prince/Princess Charming. Then what happens? You realize that you need *more* to hold on to that transitory but marvelous state of BEING you treasure so highly. The basic flaw in

the formula is that if you make your state of being—
the goal of the whole thing—contingent on *anything*,
it becomes impossible to have that state of being for
more than a few moments. Until the mind tells you
that you need to go out and DO some more, so you can
HAVE a little more, and get back some of that feeling of
BEING secure/at peace/fulfilled/happy.

The reason you can never win using the Deferred
Life Plan is that the plan itself is fundamentally flawed
in at least two ways:

⬦   First, the *goal* of the game—to do whatever it
takes to create a feeling of security: personally,
spiritually, financially, and socially—points you
in the wrong direction. You end up doing things
that give you a temporary 'hit' of what you are
after, but it disappears almost immediately and
you need another 'fix' of recognition, money,
toys, or victory.

⬦   The second flaw is in the *principle* of the plan,
which is: *repress now—relax later.* Work hard
now, suppress your needs of body, mind, and
spirit, focus on looking good and getting ahead,
and then one day you'll be able to relax and
take care of your self. The downside, which is
not even in the small print, is: *Nobody ever
wins the Default Game.* No matter how well
you do, it will never be enough. The anxiety
never really goes away. Trying to be a winner,
you repress the Now, but the Later—when you
are supposed to be able to relax—never comes.
Ironically, you end up like the guy in Jesus'

story who "gained the whole world (you could say invested himself completely in the Deferred Life Plan) but lost his soul."

Dr. John: One Day Soon ...

A participant at one of our Intensives, Dr. John, a middle-aged Medical Director of a well-known insurance company, was struggling with this issue. "You want to know how I make it through each day with all the crap that goes on in my job? I just hunker down, work as hard as I can—twelve to fourteen hours a day—and remind myself that one day it'll be better. One day I will be able to relax. I've got a mortgage to pay, several cars to maintain, kids to put through school. I can't stop now. I've got to keep running flat out, like the hamster inside the wheel. But one day I'll retire. Just a few more years! *Then* I'll be able to have a life!"

At this, Joe, one of the other participants, became activated. First, some background: Joe had, for many of his teenage years, been a Mafia runner, which evolved into being a heavy heroin user and dealer on the streets of Cleveland. He still carried the rugged good looks and engaging street patois that had served him so well for so long in that other world. Now, clean for twelve years and a successful entrepreneur, he had become a personal savior to hundreds of addicted men and women who he led to sobriety. He got up, walked over to Dr. John, fixed him with a powerful stare and said—with a voice straight out of *The Sopranos*, "Man, you got da needle in your arm as bad as any friggin' junkie lyin' in a doorway. You think you gonna wait for six years and *den* you can get your life back? Man, you dyin' right now, only you can't see it! You a dead man walkin.' If you ain't got a life right *now*, buddy, in dis moment, you ain't *never* gonna have a life!"

Ever so slowly, as he stared into Joe's intense eyes fixing him, Dr. John's countenance softened from the grim mask and furrowed brow that was his 'game face.' Tears began to run silently down his cheeks. After a few moments, he said, "You're right, Joe. You're right. Thanks, man." They hugged, the dam broke, and he began to sob. Minutes later, as he came out of the deep emotions cleansing him, he looked up at the group, "Hey, guys. I'm a *doctor*, for Pete's sake. I know what's happening to me. My cardiologist said last month that the way things are going I might not live to see my retirement. He said I'm killing myself. I guess my strategy isn't working." (Gentle chuckles rippled around the room.)

To finish the story, Dr. John went back to his company, having made a commitment to find a way to *take his life back*—before he retired. Among the most significant things he did were these: He threw away all his (unread) medical journals, which had been hanging over his head like a Damocletian sword since he had left his practice to become an administrator.

"I've been feeling guilty for years about not keeping up with my profession. Now I'm admitting the truth: I'm not a doctor any longer; I'm a medical manager, an executive. That's not only enough, it's great!" He started going home at 5:30pm instead of 7:30 or 8:00. He began to take regular walks with his wife and just hang out with his family. He softened—a little bit—when it came to pushing people for superhuman results. The bottom line: "I have started actually enjoying going to work again, and my people are reporting that they do, too. I think this insight has added years—and deep enjoyment—to my life."

Dr. John, like many of us, had turned his job into a life *consuming* project, hoping it would turn out to be a life-*giving* project. It wasn't working. Ironically, he was sacrificing himself on the altar of his job and praying that it wouldn't kill him.

They Told Us Wrong

The Deferred Life strategy is by far the most popular one we find. You may have a version of it going on in your head. You need to understand that it's doomed to failure. All the hard work, all the effort you are investing is *on top of* something that is 'off,' and which is usually being ignored. What's off is the flawed logic chain on which it's based. It's like the same logic I used to hear on our ship in the Navy when someone would complain about how bad things were. Actually, as anyone who has been in the military knows, griping is just a part of the game. If someone didn't have a gripe, the assumption was they were out of touch with reality! Whenever anybody made a serious gripe, the 'lifers'—people who were career sailors—some of whom were trapped in the cycle we are describing here, would give this advice: "Ship for six and hope for change." Translation: Sign up for six more years and maybe things will be different down the road. Yeah, right.

More of the same, only different, isn't going to get you where you want to go. The strategy, "Work harder at A (the job), so I can get lots of B (what you believe you want and need), and that will get me C (a sense of fulfillment and security)" is doomed to failure. With that model, *you can never get past* B. As you'll see in a minute, you need to *bring* C *to* A and forget about B.

Stuff: How Much Is Enough?

One key element in the Deferred Life Plan is accumulating 'stuff' to buffer yourself from the possibility of bad things happening to you, and as a substitute for that state of peace you are wanting to experience. Throwing yourself into your job now for a personal security and fulfillment later—is usually *conscious*. Surrounding yourself with 'stuff' is usually *unconscious*. You don't think of it as collecting *stuff,* you think of it as 'having the necessities of life.' You are then able to busy yourself in taking care of your stuff. You count your stuff. You track how your stuff is doing. You polish and clean your stuff. All the while, secretly hoping having enough stuff will bring you the sense of security you seek.

One senior executive, Doug, a guy with a net worth of a little over $2,000,000 at the time, told me at his Intensive, "I just need to put a little more away, then I can relax." I asked him to name an exact dollar figure which, if put away, would allow him to relax. He got out his calculator, doodled for a few minutes on a piece of paper, then looked up and said, with an amazed look, "John, I don't think there is *any* number that will be enough. It'll *never* be enough. I'll always need or want more." With this realization he went home resolving to find a way to enjoy what he had while he had it, rather than strain for what he didn't have. He discovered the root meaning of the word 'enjoy' which is to 'insert joy' or 'bring joy' or 'put joy *into* something', not hope you will *find* it there. The joy comes from inside you, not out there in the stuff or the circumstances surrounding you.

Breaking The Cycle

To bring this home, I invite you to do a simple exercise. For a few minutes jot down your responses to this topic: *If you were living the perfect life ten years from now, what would be present?* Seriously, take five minutes and do it now before reading on.

Over the years I have done this exercise with thousands of men and women literally around the world. Which of the three (DOING, HAVING, BEING) would you imagine gets the least attention during the five minutes? Right. BEING. People speak a lot about what they hope to be DOING (good work, having fun on weekends, loving their children, etc.), as well as what they hope to HAVE (a boat, a life partner who loves them, a house in the country, a job that they love, etc.)—but very little about what they hope to BE in ten years, very little about that state of peace or fulfillment or security.

Chapter Sixteen

The Real You, Out There in the World

People's tendency not to think about the BEING aspect of their Deferred Life Plan is ironic, because it's the BEING that's the goal for all the DOING and HAVING. It's the reason for everything, the ultimate purpose or objective of the time and effort.

The Whole Life Now Plan

In taking on Question 4: WHAT CALLS ME? I am proposing a radical shift to a completely different approach. We are talking about a way that turns the DO-so-as-to-HAVE-which-one-day-gets-me-to-BE model on its head. It's like what you do when you turn a sock inside out (which, interestingly, is the root meaning of the Aramaic word for 'repent'). Everything changes— significantly. What used to be down is now up, what used to make sense doesn't anymore, what it was all about is now an interesting but trivial afterthought. What I am suggesting is that you start over, reversing the formula for success. It will feel like going backward—or so the old game would have you believe—but if you do, an entirely new world of possibilities will open up for you.

As contemporary philosopher Carl Bard has put it, *"No one can go back and create a completely new beginning, but anyone can start from now and create a completely new ending."* It means starting with who you ARE and letting what you DO flow from that place, reducing the importance of what you get from the world.

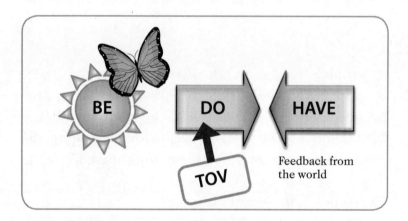

Going For Tov

Going back to my roots again, if you take a look at the creation story in the Biblical material (Genesis) you will see that there is an example there of the BE → DO → HAVE process I am proposing. (I'll be translating from the original language—and taking some literary license, but we have to do that to get the essence of any ancient material.) At one point the story goes something like this: "Then the Lord created the oceans, looked, and saw that they were good." Now the word translated there as 'good' is *tov* in the original language. Actually, 'good' is a somewhat misleading and inadequate translation for the concept inherent in the word *tov*.

A much more powerful translation would go like this: "Then the Lord created the oceans, looked, and said, 'Oh, yeah! *That's* what I'm talking about! *That's* what I had in mind! Oooh, man, it feels good to have done that! Those oceans are a piece of who I am out there in the world where you can see it. You want to learn something about *me*? Look at my oceans. That's *tov*. That's 'me' made manifest!"

Tov is 'The Real You, out there in the world.' *Tov* is something that happens when an aspect of who you are, down deep, close to your essence, your soul or spirit or charism, gets expressed out into the world where it has an impact.

Tov is what happens when something you create—a moment with a colleague or friend, a phone call, an interaction, a project, a budget, a meeting—is a manifestation of who you truly are. It's when something you DO reflects the highest and best of who you ARE. It's not about looking good, or even about the quality or perfection of what you have created. It's knowing that the act of bringing it into existence took all of your charism, all of what lives at the core of who you ARE. *Tov* is what happens when you unleash and fully express your charism, the best and deepest of who you are, out there into the world.

Asa: *Filling the House*

One day I walked in the back door of the house and heard my son Asa playing the piano in the living room. Now, I know I'm his dad, but to say "Asa was playing the piano" is like saying "Shakespeare was doing some writing." A naturally gifted musician, Asa was playing one of his favorite pieces, Rachmaninov's energetic and powerful *Prelude in D Minor.* As I stood listening quietly in the back hall, I could picture him on the other side of the wall, sitting at the grand piano, which took up most of the living room, his fingers flying over the keyboard. The whole house was reverberating.

Then something dawned on me. I realized that the house was not reverberating with the piano; it wasn't even reverberating with Rachmaninov. *The house was reverberating with* <u>*Asa*</u>. That piano, as grand as it was, would just sit there, and that Rachmaninov piece would just be a few sheets of music with dots and lines on paper, until Asa sat down, brought all of who he was to the moment, and poured his soul into that keyboard. Sitting at that piano, Asa was not so much *doing* anything as he was simply fully *being* himself, which meant that what happened—his *doing*—was a manifestation, an expression of who he is.

Similarly, my daughter Emma is a dancer, along with several other kinds of self-expression. When she dances, she is not trying to impress anyone; she is not dancing to get compliments or positive feedback. *She dances because she's Emma*—and Emma dances. The dancing is just a manifestation of who she is. Asa plays piano. Emma dances. They simply fully express who they are; and what happens next—what they *get from the world* as a result, like feedback—is almost an afterthought. The whole thing gets turned around into: Be → Do → Have.

What if you began to see your job as simply your 'instrument,' and your job description as your 'score,' both waiting for you to step in and bring them to life by putting who you *are* into them. Once again, letting what you DO be an expression of the best of who you ARE.

Changing Your Major

It was September, 1957, and I was a seventeen year old senior year at Thomas Jefferson High School in Richmond, VA. On October 4th, the Russians launched Sputnik, that tiny silver ball that was the first human-made object to circumnavigate the earth in space—and the space race was on. As a senior, it was time to figure out what to do after high school. Heck, I didn't know! I didn't even know how to start figuring it out.

As I recall, no one at home or at school asked me what I wanted to do, or what subjects I really enjoyed. My high school guidance counselors gave me aptitude tests and vocational interest assessments and seemed thrilled at the results. "Johnny, you blew the top off the scores on those visual tests, the verbal tests, and the logic tests, plus you show a remarkable aptitude for the physical sciences, something America needs right now. The Russians are beating us in the space race, and you would make a wonderful engineer. Why don't you give that a try when you go to college?"

"Sure, why not?" I said, not having a better idea, and off to Roanoke College I went, enrolled as an Engineering student. Roanoke is a liberal arts school—and a really good one, too, by the way. For that reason, when I started in September 1958, I was taking, along with my Engineering and Math classes, courses like World Civilization, Psychology, and Philosophy.

One day about half-way through the second semester, I remember realizing that, while I enjoyed my Engineering Drawing and Physics classes, I *really* enjoyed my World Civ and Psych classes. Couldn't wait to get to them. Loved the reading each night. Although there wasn't much of it as a result of my being on the varsity Swim Team and the Honor Council in my spare time, all my conversations in the Hub were not about the *hard* sciences but about the *social* sciences. In those classes, *it felt like I already knew the material.* It was as if all the lectures, the reading, the bull sessions, were giving me labels for things that were there, inside me, waiting for me to discover them. In History, taught by Homer Bast, the most wonderful teacher I ever had, I would read a chapter *once* and all the dates, who did what to whom, and why, were all embedded in my mind.

So, one day I walked into Dean Don Sutton's office and said I wanted to change my major. Being a wise reader of students' inner worlds, he pushed back to make sure I was serious, and then said, "Of course, Johnny," and made the necessary changes in my schedule for the next semester. Four years later, I had earned enough credits to claim both History and Philosophy as majors—with a minor in Psychology.

Looking back on that seemingly simple decision—to change my major—it strikes me as being something that all human beings must confront at some point in their lives.

- ⬥ Am I on the right track?
- ⬥ Is this the work my soul wants me to be doing?
- ⬥ Is it *tov*?
- ⬥ How will I know?

How To Tell When It's Tov

How can you tell whether what you are learning or doing or *thinking about doing* is 'right' for you? Try these simple tests:

- ⬥ When you think about doing _____, or are doing it, do you find yourself getting excited?
- ⬥ Does your eye seek out books and magazines and journals about _____ in a bookstore?
- ⬥ When you pick up a magazine or journal in that field, are you eager to get into it?
- ⬥ When you read about _____, or attend a lecture, or get into a conversation with an __ _____ expert, do you find it really easy to remember what was said? Does _____ 'stick' with you with little or no effort?
- ⬥ When there *is* hard work in _____, do you experience it as fulfilling and even enjoyable?
- ⬥ Do you find yourself looking for opportunities to talk about _____ with your friends and/or family members?

Several years ago, in response to my question about which book I ought to write, an agent told me, "John, write your book on the subject you could talk about every day of your life for the next three years and not get bored."

Isn't that a great one! What would you be excited to learn about, talk about, maybe even teach about, for the next few years and not get bored? Your thoughtful response to THAT question will take you close to the creative core of what you ought to be doing with your life. The answer is usually something that can be started right where you are. In that same job, with those same people. Sometimes you might discover you need to 'change your major,' but more often than not, it's about what you re discover inside yourself to *bring* to that work that puts you in the right place, doing the right thing.

Claudia: The Dragon Lady

During a senior leadership team workshop I was facilitating a few years ago, there was an amazing example of this. The organization was headed up by an Executive Director—we'll call her Claudia—who had a reputation for being The Dragon Lady, as she was called not so affectionately, behind her back. Tough, unyielding, abrupt, direct to the point of meanness sometimes, she ruled her staff with an iron hand, driving them hard to be the best, rarely handing out kudos or words of encouragement.

At the point in the workshop when we were going into the BE → DO → HAVE model she stopped me and said, "Okay, John, enough of this airy-fairy @#$%! We've got work to do around this place! We haven't got time for all this @#&*#$%." (Claudia had a vocabulary that would have made some of my buddies in the Navy blush, so I've cleaned it up for the book.)

"Claudia," I said, "Okay, I hear you, but let me ask you a question: If someone gave you a million dollars and you didn't have to do this work, what would you do with yourself?"

She thought for a moment and said, "Well, I don't see what that's got to do with the leadership development work we're doing here, but I guess I'd go home and play with my grandkids."

"Just stay with me for a minute," I said. "Tell us what playing with your grandkids looks like. Give us the video replay of a day of being with them. Start before they come in the door. What do you do? Oh, and would someone in the group start to write down what Claudia says on the easel pad? Thanks."

"Okay, first I get the house ready."

"What do you mean?" I ask.

"Well, I make sure the house is full of things they like to do, that there is food for them, and learning type games, and that it's safe. And I get myself ready."

"How do you get yourself ready—and why?"

"Hey, being a grandma is important work! You have to be mentally and emotionally ready. I mean they have needs—each one is different, and I want to make sure I can be there for them."

"What does that mean?"

"It means I want to be the kind of grandma that

they deserve. I want to not miss a chance to help them if they need me." (Remember, all this is getting written down.)

"Okay, they're starting to come in the door, what do you do now?"

"I open the door and welcome them as warmly as I can. For the little ones I get down on my knees to greet them at their own level. I give each one a big hug and tell each one how happy I am to see them." (She starts to get emotional at this point.)

"Yes. I can picture you doing that! Then what do you do all day with them?"

"Oh, mainly, I make sure they have whatever they need, food, toys, tools. I look for those magic moments to teach them something, or if they need help with an art project or whatever, I offer to give them a hand. When they get bored, I help them think of other ideas of what they could do. The day flies by, actually, and I am really sorry to see them go."

"How does the day end?"

"Their mom or dad comes to the door, but I hold each one real close (she cries a little as she says this), tell them what a joy it was to be with them for the day, and say I can't wait till they come back."

"Not exactly like work, huh?" I said.

She chuckles through her tears. "Not exactly."

"Isn't that a shame that work is so different; but maybe not, Claudia. Would someone read off the newsprint what she said? Now, as you hear each one, Claudia, I want you to look to see whether there is anything from how you are with your grandchildren might translate into you as the leader of this organization."

One of the VPs begins to read what she has written:

- ⋄ I get myself prepared.
- ⋄ I make sure the house is ready, that they have everything they need—to learn and have fun.
- ⋄ I greet them individually at the door.
- ⋄ I meet them on their level.
- ⋄ I give them hugs (make warm contact).
- ⋄ I look for 'teaching moments' when they are open to learning.
- ⋄ I make sure they have what they need.
- ⋄ If they get bored, I help them find something else to do.
- ⋄ I express my love to each one when they leave.
- ⋄ I tell them how wonderful it was to be with them—and that I can't wait to see them again.

Bringing Grandma To Work

Claudia stared at the newsprint for what seemed like a long time. Several of the VPs were visibly moved, too, by the implications of what they saw on the easel.

After a while Claudia said quietly, "What you're telling me, John, is that I could bring my Grandma to work!" Long pause. (Her managers were silently mouthing: "Yes! Yes! Please!") "Wow, what a concept. I never would have thought."

"Yes, Claudia. What if you have just re defined what it might mean to be the leader of this organization? What if this is your new job description? What if you came to work with the same frame of mind as the one you just described to us? What if your role as Executive Director was to ..." and I read off the newsprint, making a few small adjustments:

- ⋄ make sure you and the office are ready.
- ⋄ personally greet each person you see and act as if he or she is special.
- ⋄ make sure people have what they need to enjoy a productive day.
- ⋄ look for opportunities to teach or help if asked.
- ⋄ assist people to find interesting (important) things to do.
- ⋄ thank them at the end of the day.

Claudia sat, stunned. "Oh, my goodness." She was speechless. Again, after a long while she mused quietly, "Well, team, I guess I've got some work to do. If I have been mean or insensitive to you all, I apologize. I thought I had to be hard and tough to motivate you. I believed that if I were soft and weak, people would walk all over me. I can only imagine what it's been like for you. I know I'm known as The Dragon Lady to you. (Some team members shifted uneasily in their seats.) After this little exercise, I can see why! Okay, let's see if you can help me bring my grandma to work. Thanks, John, for this experience. I can see it now: I will be more effective if I just practice being who I am down deep inside—a grandma—and let what I do as leader flow from her."

A lightness came over her face and she beamed at her team. "This just could be fun!" A few months later, she and her team reported major positive shifts in Claudia's leadership style—and in the team's effectiveness. When I walked in one day and said hello to the receptionist, she smiled a big smile and said, "John, Grandma's in the building!"

Chapter Seventeen

The Sweet Spot

Resolving The Three 'Pulls'

What *calls* you is different from what *pulls* you. Drawing on the work of our old friend, Sigmund Freud, I say there are three 'pulls' on you virtually all day every day, three aspects that make demands on you—and rightfully so.

- ⋄ Self—what *you* need in a given situation
- ⋄ Others—what those around you need
- ⋄ Cause—what the larger context is calling for

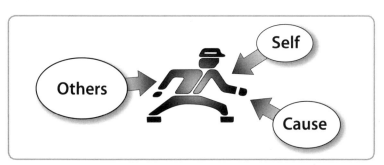

At any given time, one of these three pulls 'wins', and we 'lean' that way, paying attention to that one and disregarding the other two. This is not a bad thing, it's a human thing, but if we make a *habit* of attending to the same one at the expense of the other two, bad things start to happen. They are like traps, because they ensnare us, and make it hard or impossible for us to move, to be and do what is called for.

For instance, in a relationship, there is what *you* need or want, what your *partner* needs or wants, and then there is what your *relationship* needs or wants. In a work setting, there is what *you* need (say in a meeting or decision-making process), what your *colleagues* who are involved need, and what the *team* or the *organization* needs or wants. How you balance these pulls has a lot to do with your effectiveness and with your degree of purpose, power, and peace.

Most people tend to pay too much attention way too often to one pull to the exclusion of the others. Over time, this results in frustration—in you and in others—working much harder than necessary, creating conflicts as you go along and, in general, being blocked from being effective and/or at peace. Think of theses tendencies as *habits*.

The Narcissistic Habit   (Me, Me, And Only Me)

If you attend only and always to what you need, and neglect completely what the *others* around you need and what *life* is calling for, you end up becoming disconnected. You lose touch with other people and with the wider or larger context, both of which have legitimate things to say to you, both of which have guidance for you. "Someone all wrapped up in himself," as my Grandmother Scherer used to say, "makes a mighty small package." If we are caught in the Narcissistic Habit, we can get a lot done, achieve a lot and become quite successful, but there is a slight downside.

Remember the old Greek story of Narcissus? He was a really good looking warrior who was so self-absorbed that he sat for hours by the water, looking at his reflection and marveling at how attractive he was. One day 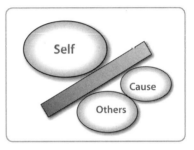 as he leaned over to get an even closer look, he fell in, and, weighed down by his heavy armor, drowned.

When you are in the grip of this habit, nothing matters but your own needs. What the other people in the situation need is not important to you, nor is the context or the larger mission. As with each of the three habits, there is an upside (otherwise no one would do them!) and, unfortunately, a downside as well.

The Upside of the Narcissistic Habit

◇ You tend to look good—unless people get too close.

◇ Your own needs are more likely to get met.

◇ It gives you the illusion of control and freedom.

However, as in all aspects of life (remember the Polarity Map on Page 178) there is also a potential downside. No matter how hard you work at taking care of yourself to the exclusion of other people and the mission or context, these things are also highly predictable:

The Downside of the Narcissistic Habit

⋄ Eventually people will no longer trust you—or want to work with you.

⋄ Your decisions, since they all come from the mind of the same person (you), will not always be as wise as ones made with input from others.

⋄ At some point you will encounter a situation where life is calling on you to give up something you are desperate to hold on to (like credit for success, turf, staff, etc). If you can't put yourself second, you will fall down the ladder of success.

If we can't put ourselves second or third—even for a moment—we will fail, often dramatically.

The Martyr Habit   (*You, You, And Only You*)

If, on the other hand, you always attend only to what other people need to the exclusion of what you need and what life is calling for, you become mired in the Martyr Habit. Maybe you know this one. I do. My Somebody Training and Autopilot—now hardened into my Con—tells me not to be selfish or self-centered, to always put other people first. "Forget your own needs, John. You'll survive. Make do with what is there. And don't worry about what life is calling for. *The* most important thing for you to do is meet that other person's needs."

If you are in a relationship with a Martyr and you ask, "Where would you like to go to dinner tonight, dear?" what will the Martyr partner say back? Right! "Wherever *you* want to go, sweetheart; that's where *I* want to go." The message is "I don't matter" or "I don't even have any needs or wants" or "My job is to meet *your* needs." The Martyr is so tuned into the other person's life that they often have no awareness of their own.

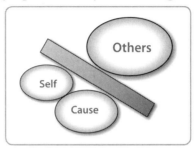

Martyrs come in for a lot of jokes, but there could well be one down there inside you if your Somebody Training taught you to put other people first. I can still recall my Grandmother telling me, "Johnny, you come *third*. God comes first, other people come second, and then, way down the line, you come third."

In the workplace, certain departments tend to form themselves around this stance, units who have the assignment to support other groups. HR, IT, and sometimes Finance can fall into this habit. "We're here to take care of *you*." There is a lot to be said for that approach. The upside of the Martyr Habit is that it is very socially acceptable, even rewarded.

The Upside of the Martyr Habit

⋄ Taking care of others is socially acceptable and often rewarded.

⋄ You look like you care.

⋄ There can be great satisfaction in seeing other people benefit from your focused effort to contribute and problem-solve.

There is also a downside:

The Downside of the Martyr Habit

⋄ If you fail to care for yourself to some extent in the process, you are likely to collapse, and then not be able to care for anyone.

⋄ If you fail to consider the Mission or Context or Cause, you may do things that are not appropriate.

After a while, the people around you want to throw up. They want you to get real, to want something for yourself. Nobody can live every moment for everyone else. Even Jesus and Buddha, each of whom has been seen as 'a man for others', took time to recharge and renew themselves.

Put Your Own Oxygen Mask On First

If you get on an airplane, just before you take off, the flight attendant will say something like this: "In the unlikely event of a loss of cabin pressure, an oxygen mask will drop from the compartment above you. Pull the mask down and place it firmly over your mouth and nose, securing the strap behind your head. Even though the bag is not inflating, oxygen IS flowing. If you are traveling with a small child or someone who needs assistance (here's the clincher) *secure your own mask first before rendering assistance.*" Duh. If you are gasping for air, how can you help anyone else?

Mother Teresa Took Breaks

A fascinating story about Mother Teresa comes to mind here. As I heard it, a magazine reporter was visiting with her at the Missionaries of Charity center in Calcutta, India. It was around 7:00pm and the two of them were talking quietly when one of the Sisters came in and said, with some urgency in her voice, "Mother Teresa, come quickly! We are having trouble at the gate!" The two of them—Mother Teresa and the magazine reporter—got up and went to the gate where they saw hundreds of people on the street outside, straining to get in. Joining the several Sisters who were doing their best to shut and lock the huge door, with Mother Teresa herself leaning into it, they managed to push against the sea of humanity pressing to get in and to lock the gate. As they walked back across the courtyard to the room to continue their conversation, the reporter, incredulous, said, "Mother Teresa! I can't believe I saw what I just saw! I thought you were here to *help* those people, not toss them out on the street!" "My good sir," she replied, "if my Sisters and I don't close that gate every evening to get our own rest and spiritual sustenance, this place would close in three days."

If you are out of balance on this one, you will end up not only unable to help anyone, but potentially angry at the ones you are intending to help. Well-meaning, self-sacrificing clergy, nurses, therapists, and social workers can easily find themselves resenting their members, patients, and clients. In the workplace, it is not unusual for the 'service' departments to feel unappreciated and ticked off at the other departments they are supposed to be supporting.

There has to be a workable creative tension between meeting your own needs and helping meet the needs of others.

The True Believer/Fanatic Habit (*The Cause, The Cause, Only The Cause*)

There is another habit that can trip you up: putting the Mission, 'the Cause' ahead of everything else all the time, disregarding your own needs and the needs of others. As someone who served in the military, I understand this principle, and there were times when everything—including the safety of myself and my people—came second to completing the mission. We have all had experiences where we worked hard to complete a project, putting all else aside. "It's a good thing," as Martha Stewart would say. Those moments

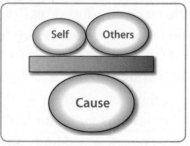

are actually exhilarating, but to do that *all the time,* sacrificing your own well-being and that of others— now that's another matter altogether.

True Believers (we also call them Fanatics) come in all kinds and flavors. They are people who put the mission or the cause or the larger purpose ahead of themselves and other people. Every successful entrepreneur has had to be a fanatic about her or his idea. It's all about the Mission. When we approve of their idea, we applaud their dedication to the Mission, and call them great leaders and social innovators. Gandhi, Martin Luther King, Jr., Sojourner Truth, and Lech Walesa are a few who come to mind. When we *don't* approve of their position, we call them fanatics, and Osama bin Laden, Saddam Hussein, and Joseph Stalin come to mind.

The Upside of the True Believer/Fanatic Habit

- Every important cause or movement needs a 'first wave' willing to sacrifice themselves 'on the beaches' for the principle they believe in so strongly. People like Moses, Jesus, Buddha, Joan of Arc, Mother Teresa, as well as those who have given their lives in movements throughout history, all sacrificed themselves for the Cause.

- True Believers and Fanatics tend to get a lot done, attract followers, and have great impact.

- There can be great satisfaction—and even great lasting value—in making a large difference in the world.

The Downside of the True Believer/Fanatic Habit

- Fanatics have no true friends, only potential converts to the cause.

- 'Workaholic' is a word that comes to mind.

- At some point, other people need to make their own connection to the cause to move forward and expand the base for impact. They can't always follow you.

✧ It is very difficult for the True Believer to avoid over identifying the success of the movement with their own success. Many causes are done in by the ego and/or the human foibles of the True Believer who started it off.

By focusing entirely on The Cause to the exclusion of yourself and other people, you isolate yourself. It becomes virtually impossible to have any kind of relationships *except in terms of your cause*. You must know people who just have a 'thing.' No matter what the conversation is about, sooner or later you know it will come around to be about their 'thing.'

Angie's Thing

Several years ago a good friend called and said she wanted to come over to talk about something. This in itself was a little strange because Angie (we'll call her) was the kind of friend who would just come in the back door and say, "I'm here! I'm making myself a cup of tea!"

I said okay, and she came over and said, "I'd like to speak with you in the living room, if I may." Again, a little strange.

"Okay," I said, and went to sit down.

She pulled out a briefcase (another strange thing) and, looking at me deeply, said, "John, what could you do if you had more money in your life?"

I recall being a little surprised and saying something like, "Angie, you know money isn't a big deal to me. I like having it because it allows me to do some things I might not otherwise, but it doesn't motivate me at all."

"Yes, but think about what you could do if you had more money!"

"Angie, you're not hearing me. It's not the way I think. You know that."

"Yes, but think about what you could do if you had more money, John!"

Then 'the shoe dropped' and it dawned on me what this was about. "Oh, I get it, Angie! We're in a multi-level marketing conversation, aren't we? Just tell us what the product is—I'm sure it's a good one—and I'll buy some, but I don't want to be a distributor."

"Yes, but think about what you could do if you had more money, John!" Geez, it was like a broken record. (Which I understand is one of the techniques taught for such situations.)

"Angie!" I said, starting to get ticked off, "I want to be your friend. I do *not* want to be in your 'downline'!"

"Yes, but John, think about what you could do if you had more money!"

"Angie, you are not hearing me. Stop The Pitch you are here to make. I am not interested! Just stop!"

"Okay, John, but let me leave these cassettes with you."

"Angie," I interrupted, "do not leave those cassettes with me. Give them to somebody who is going to listen to them."

Closing her briefcase and starting for the door, she lobbed one last shot over her shoulder on the way out: "Okay, but think about what you could do if you had more money!"

What do you think has happened to our friendship? Right. It's gone, replaced by her cause, her 'thing', her

246 *Five Questions That Change Everything*

John Scherer

Mission. If she walked up to you right now, she would not be seeing *you*; she would be seeing *a potential distributor* in her 'game.' Remember the concept in Question 2: WHAT AM I BRINGING? *Where you are coming from*—what your deepest agenda is—trumps everything else and determines *where you end up.*

Where They All Matter: *The Sweet Spot*

What you need to have access to is a way to respond to all three 'pulls' at the same time, and do it in a way that not only doesn't cost you energy, but actually increases

it. I call it the Sweet Spot. If you have ever played a sport with a bat, racquet, or club, you know what I am talking about. Hit a tennis ball in the exact center of your racquet

The Sweet Spot

and you will have tremendous accuracy and pace, with very little effort. Even as a soccer player, I recall that feeling of really thumping the ball with just the right spot on my foot.

What if there were a way to live and work all day, every day, in such a place? It is possible, even simple. You are in the Sweet Spot when you are fully engaged in that School of Life 'assignment' I described on Page 5. You are in The Sweet Spot, when you are putting your charism to work in:

⋄ an act of complete and joyful self-expression— regardless of the outcome or response from the world (this nurtures YOU),

⬧ which contributes to the highest and best of any OTHERS involved, and

⬧ is in alignment with what LIFE itself is calling for.

The Zone

The Sweet Spot can be recognized by a sense of maximum effectiveness and deep fulfillment. Have you ever been on the job and worked really hard all day, yet gone home energized? Sure you have. Ever done next to nothing all day long and gone home exhausted? Sure you have. I think what is happening in both those instances has to do with how much you were working within the Sweet Spot. Once again, it is stepping into this moment, this conversation, this phone call, this meeting, looking for how to attend to all three: Yourself, Others, and The Cause. It means doing what I have called 'going for *tov*.'

Being in the Sweet Spot or having *tov* is not about having a certain kind of job; it's about bringing who you ARE *to* that job. I'll bet you have known engineers, hairdressers, nurses, teachers, parents, executives, bus drivers, car salesmen, maybe even trash collectors who seem to know this Sweet Spot/ *tov* space. When all three 'pulls' are being addressed, even to some extent, you are in the Sweet Spot or *tov* space. Athletes, singers, dancers, runners, and artists call it The Zone.

What Life Is Calling For

Put all three of these 'pulls' together, and you are asking yourself, "In this moment, what is LIFE calling for from me?" Life: that larger context. The one that surrounds everything else in the equation: your Con, your 'stuff', the other person's 'stuff', the circumstances, your considerations, all the reasons it probably won't work or will be difficult or will make you look bad, the relationship, even the Mission or Cause itself. LIFE encompasses *all of that*. Everything that is important in that moment gets enfolded, embraced, in what LIFE itself needs from you in this moment.

Tov. The Sweet Spot. The Zone. Responding to what LIFE is calling for. These are just different words for the same phenomenon. They all describe that place your soul yearns for all day, every day.

Finding Your Tov

If you are ready to discover—or re discover—your *tov*, here are a few questions that will begin to take you closer to that inner territory where your charism is waiting for a chance to show itself:

- ◇ What are you really good at that you never learned—you just always seemed to have it in you?

- ◇ What would you be willing to do, even if you didn't get paid for it?

- ◇ What do you get lost in when you do it, losing track of time?

- ◇ What would the people who know you best say you are good at?

- ◇ What's so easy for you that you can't figure out why other people think it's a big deal?

- ⬧ What daydreams about what to do with your life keep floating through your mind—and haven't gone away?

- ⬧ What do you do that gives you energy when you do it? What saps or drains your energy when you do it?

- ⬧ What were some of the things you wanted to be when you grew up?

The bigger question is, now that you have become reacquainted with all this great stuff inside you, what are you going to DO with it? Where are you going to 'aim' your Self?

Chapter Eighteen

What Calls You From Outside

Now that you have discerned what is moving *inside* you that demands to be expressed, it's time to revisit the *external* aspect of what calls you. To get at it, ask yourself these questions:

- If you just walked into a room, without having to think about it, without your having to DO anything, what impact would you hope your simple presence would have on people around you?
- What would you set yourself to if you knew it would not fail?
- What deep need does the world have that you would give anything to see met or addressed?
- What is something you deeply want to see happening in the world three generations from now *because you had been alive*—and no one knows you had anything to do with it?[*]

[*] This powerful question is from a good friend and colleague, Dwight Frindt.

Dwight's question introduces a crucial aspect to the whole process of unleashing yourself: Why are you doing whatever you are doing? Are you hoping or angling to get something out of it? Probably. Don't forget your Con, diagrammed on Page 187. There has to be something larger than your Con to get you paradoxically outside of yourself so that you can bring more of your true self to what you are doing. Interestingly, that's the root meaning of our word 'ecstasy', which means literally 'to stand outside yourself.' When you are in The Sweet Spot, the Zone, Going for Tov, you will experience a kind of ecstasy, a joy, a sense of excitement and being on your 'edge.'

What could be large enough to call you out of your Con and into that space of joyful self-expression? How about something so important to LIFE that you would want to see what you are doing contribute to it, even if no one ever knew you were contributing to it. Now, that would be worth going for, wouldn't it? This means seeing beyond this specific task that is engaging your energy to the larger intention that has gripped your soul.

The Tae Kwan Do Metaphor

One of my good friends, Eli Davis, is a Black Belt in Tae Kwan Do, and a graduate of the Intensive based on FIVE QUESTIONS. We were talking recently about the concept of *focus*. "Wherever you put your focus, that's where your energy will *stop*," he explained to me. "In attempting to break a board, for instance, if you focus on *the board*, your strike will come to a screeching stop when it hits the top edge of the board. More than likely, your hand will either bounce off, or become injured from the impact. To break the board, you need to focus on something *beyond* the board. The breaking of the board then becomes just something that happened *on the way through* to your ultimate focus. This is what you would call a Greater Purpose, John."

The Greater Purpose of this Book: The 'So That' Inquiry
Let's work with a real, present example: What is my writing this book really about? What is the purpose of this book? Could it be to:

- ◇ become a household name? (With a name like John Jacob Scherer IV, I'm not sure that's such a great idea.)
- ◇ to make a lot of money? (Very few books actually do.)
- ◇ to measure up to the standard my grandfather set? (That was then, this is now. He would probably be proud of me.)
- ◇ to finally be able to relax about how I lived my life? (That either happens daily or it doesn't happen at all.)

None of these seems sufficiently large or enduring enough, given Dwight's question. None of them makes my heart sing. What if this book were just 'the board' that I encountered on the way through to my real or greater focus or intention? That's what I realized in a conversation with Jim Berquist, another friend and colleague on this path of life transforming work. Here's how it unfolded.

I called him and said, "Jim, I'm feeling hung up in writing my FIVE QUESTIONS book. It's almost done, but I have a feeling something is not quite right with where I am coming from as I write it, and I want it to come from the truest place possible in me."

"Okay, John. Thanks for asking. Says something about the integrity you want to have in your book writing process. It won't take long. Maybe five minutes."

"Great, Jim! I'm ready."

"What do you want for your book?" he started out.

"Well, I would want people all over the world to be reading it."

"Done!" Jim announced. "Let's say your book has taken off like a rocket. It's an international best-seller. Oprah held it up one day on her show, and the rest has been history as they say. Literally millions of people all around the world are reading the book, and using it in their lives, just as you imagined. Got that? Wonderful! Okay. What would *that* make possible?"

I thought for a moment, and said, "Then people around the world couldn't wait to get to work every morning. They'd be thinking, 'Man, what a day it's going to be today on the job! I even hope that jerk in Operations talks behind my back again, or does something equally stressing, because I learned so much last time from how we handled a similar experience. You know what? I'm a better person today precisely because of all the stuff that happens every day at work. My organization is also a better place—we are making the kind of contribution to the world that we are capable of making.' Like that," I said.

"Okay, John, then what would *that* make possible?" (I *knew* that was coming.)

A little longer pause this time. "Well, I guess we would have organizations and institutions all over the world being what *they* were capable of being. They would be living into the greater purpose that lay behind their creation in the first place."

"Okay, then what would *that* make possible, John?"

After some thought, I said, "Well, then I think we'd have a world that worked for everybody."

"Bingo! I think you're there, John! You are writing this book, not to get rich or famous, not even to have millions of people reading it, but in the service of creating a world that works for everybody. Just write from *that* place."

Isn't that amazing? By responding several times to the same little question—*What would that make possible?* you, too, can find your work taken beyond the little, ego driven, fear based, purpose that has been your default Con up to now. You can find yourself and your life placed in the context of something truly worth being up to in the world. Jim's intervention—what I call the *So That* Inquiry—was something I had done with hundreds of executives and front line people for years, but hadn't thought to apply to myself. Isn't that the way it often is? We discover that what we need to hear or see is inside us all along. We just need to be reminded of or awakened to it. I hope Five Questions is doing that for you.

Remember the premise of this book: You don't need to *change* yourself. You need to *become* yourself—and that changes everything. Now it's time to put some words around who you are and what you are about.

Chapter Nineteen

Your Greater Purpose

When you have pondered those internal and external questions long enough, drawing on the insights you discovered above, you are ready to create what I call your GPS, or Greater Purpose Statement. Your GPS will operate as a navigation aid for guiding the unfolding of your life and your work from this point on.

I like the name GPS because it reminds us of the Global Positioning System, that network of satellites that enable us to find ourselves anywhere on the earth. Your GPS here in this context does the same thing. Using it on a regular basis, you can find yourself when you are lost and don't know what to do, or when you are facing a crisis and need a sense of direction. Your GPS also puts you in touch with your charism, and points you toward what is *tov.*

What Difference Can a GPS Make?   *Waking Up*

Occasionally, our Intensive participants will say that the GPS-production process feels like a kind of trance. This is backward. What we have come to know as our normal waking state is actually much more like a trance, and the centered place from which the GPS emerges, is more connected with reality.

As you now see, we usually walk around in a default state, trapped in our Autopilot, running our Con. We perform our acts to get people to believe us (or trust us, or follow us, or respect us, etc.) without acknowledging what our hidden agenda is about. To make it work, we bring to bear all the skills and characteristics and qualities we have developed over the years and put them in the service of our default game. For ninety-nine percent of the world's population, this is totally automatic and unconscious. If that's not being in a trance, I don't know what is!

And our Con works—sort of—so we stick with it, settling for the benefits it brings us, even if those benefits don't have much joy or fulfillment or even effectiveness connected to them. We get a hit of the thing we're addicted to (*e.g.* Adoration) and we temporarily stave off the thing we're terrified of (*e.g.* Being Discarded), but the fear/addiction drivers never go away. This means we rarely have moments of lasting fulfillment and satisfaction, and rarely are as effective as we could be in working with others. *This is because what we are doing is completely self-centered.*

Waking Up

Once we wake from this trance and become aware of our habitual way of operating in the world, we can recognize its emptiness and begin looking for another, more useful, reason for being here. The Inquiry: *"If I'm not here (on the planet) to* _____ *(e.g. mine: to impress people so they will adore me and not ignore me), then why am I here?"*

That inquiry can lead to a profound internal dialogue and deep conversations with trusted friends, partners, and colleagues. The irony is that to accelerate that waking process you need to go into a deeper kind of state. To simplify things, I have condensed the soul-searching inquiry into a series of powerful questions. In this experience many people are able to bypass their patterned way of thinking and find themselves closer to another, deeper place where another, deeper *purpose* lives (and has resided for many years, waiting to be rediscovered). What calls you is *underneath* your Con and all its automatic patterns of thought.

The greater purpose that emerges is not about the specific job you should be doing. That's downstream. The GPS that emerges from this process describes a state of mind or a state of being which is much bigger than you would have ever thought of with your normal mode of thinking.

Ingredients In Your GPS

Your GPS will contain at least these three crucial elements:

✦   *Your charism*: What you are good at, the bone-deep skills and qualities that just show up wherever you are, that require no thinking or intention on your part. Anyone who is around you 'gets' these qualities or skills or characteristics. You 'walk into a room'—these come along with you. They are your favorite words on your Persona list (see Page 106. Isn't that fascinating? Buried in what you have been *trying* to be is your charism, what you simply *are* underneath the effort and anxiety!

✦   *Your Shadow Stretches:* What you know you need to practice, those ways of being from your Shadow that you must to step into if you are to continue to develop more fully into who you are. This also includes what you need to learn from your Shadow Icon (see Page 116).

✦   *Your Impossible Possibility—The So That*: The kind of effect or impact you would love to have in the world—or on those who interact with you: What you would want to see happen in any situation in which you found yourself. The 'So That Inquiry': *What does your being alive and on the earth make possible?*

Finding Your GPS   *Step 1: GPS Questions*

Pick a few of the questions from below that grab you the most and mull them over for a while. Take your time. It could take days, or weeks, or even years—but it's life-saving, life transforming work. It could be the next step in *becoming* and *unleashing* yourself, which is the aim of this book. Make the questions you select into a kind of mantra or prayer, and bring them to your consciousness off and on during the day. Make them into graphics you put on the fridge or on your desk where you can see them. Talk about them—and what is coming up in you—with a few trusted family members, friends and/or colleagues. Remember what I said in the Introduction: Your mind will generate answers to whatever question you bring it, so bring good ones!

I have filled in my own personal responses here as an illustration of how it works. As you read mine, think of what yours would be.

1. What are your Charisms (Bone deep Strengths, Capabilities, Gifts)
    ⋄ insight
    ⋄ empathy
    ⋄ courage
    ⋄ generosity
    ⋄ practical spirituality
    ⋄ authenticity
    ⋄ sense of humor
    ⋄ story-telling
    ⋄ being able to express complex concepts in ways that people 'get' them, apply them in their lives—and enjoy the experience

2. What are you meant to do here?
    ⋄ be with people at the level of their deepest need
    ⋄ love people and be a channel for the truth
    ⋄ unleash the human spirit—especially at work

⬧   put all of who I am in the service of awakening
     people and their organizations to their truest
     potential—and continue to develop myself in
     the process
⬧   transform the world at work™

3. What are you committed to?
⬧   life long development—body, mind, and spirit
⬧   being a vital, connected, loving man in service
     to the Great Work until my last breath
⬧   transforming the world at work™

4. What would you be willing to die for?
⬧   spontaneously: the rescue of almost anyone in
     need, especially loved ones
⬧   transformation of the world at work™
⬧   the creation of a world that works for everyone

5. What do you long for?
⬧   a sense of freedom to be exactly—and all of—
     who I am
⬧   an experience of belonging, of being 'at home'
     where I live
⬧   a loving life partner who yearns for me and
     accepts me just as I am
⬧   life work that demands all of who I am, and
     keeps me just past the edge of my confidence
     and competence
⬧   a world that works for everyone

6. What brings you tears of joy?
⬧   acts of courageous sacrifice (*e.g.* Frodo in *Lord*

of the Rings, or *The Song of Roland*)

 ⋄ true love expressed and received
 ⋄ being in the presence of personal breakthroughs
 ⋄ great music

7. What world condition(s) do you yearn to see changed?

 ⋄ fear-based hatred
 ⋄ greed-based leadership and fear based management
 ⋄ toxic workplaces where human beings are reduced to frightened, numb, or enraged cogs in a machine
 ⋄ the human reluctance to embrace polarities
 ⋄ the arrogance that leads us to impose our 'way' on others
 ⋄ the raping of our planet

8. What are you passionate about?

 ⋄ personal/spiritual development
 ⋄ life-long learning
 ⋄ sharing practical spiritual development principles
 ⋄ helping people create impossible possibilities

9. If you had three days left to live, what would you do?

 ⋄ write as much as I could on the next book
 ⋄ look through family photos and videos
 ⋄ call and say thank you to those who have loved me
 ⋄ make love

⋄ walk by the ocean
⋄ learn another song on my guitar
⋄ do my yoga, sing, dance, meditate, and rub the feet of my beloved

10. What are the happiest (tov) moments for you?
⋄ when I am in The Great Work with a colleague that I love and respect
⋄ watching someone break through to a new self-understanding
⋄ seeing a leadership or work team practice authenticity, purposeful action, and going for *tov*

Step 2: Writing Your Greater Purpose Statement
Now you are ready to transform those images from your Journey into a concise, powerful, and useful navigation tool, your GPS.

The GPS Formula:

_____, _____, _____, _____ (a few Stretches and maybe a charism or two from your Persona), I am _____, _____, (a couple more charisms), so that _____ (your So That, or The Impossible Possibility you seek to claim as your reality). Then make it a little *poetic* if you can.

My Own Personal GPS:
Clear, direct, worthy and real, I am a spiritual warrior, an intuitive and passionate force, unleashing the human spirit at work around the world—starting with my own.

- *Clear, direct,* and *worthy* are all Stretches for me—things that don't always come naturally in every situation.
- Seeing myself as a *force* is sometimes a Stretch, too.
- *Real, intuitive,* and *passionate* are all charisms, natural aspects of who I am.
- *Spiritual Warrior* is a powerful image for me, encapsulating everything in the GPS, calling me into all my Stretches and charisms.
- *Unleashing the human spirit at work around the world* is my Impossible Possibility, my So That.
- *Starting with my own* is an important reminder that I am in a work-in-progress just like everyone else, that I am not a finished product.

A Few Sample GPSs

To give you an idea of what a good GPS sounds like, here are a few recent examples, selected from the hundreds I have collected over the years. (I have changed the names to protect people's confidentiality.) Notice that they contain all three of the above ingredients: Stretches, Charisms, and the Impossible Possibility (So That). (I have marked which is which in bold so you can see how a GPS can get developed.)

Chris: A 43-year-old Consultant

"Confident and fully present as I promote myself, let you in, and stand in my truth (Stretches), my principled and strategic thinking (Charism) guides us to real interactions (Impossible Possibility). As I embrace fear of failure again and again (Stretch), my relaxed presence (Stretch) connects us to each other and creates organizations that get things done (Impossible Possibility)."

Pat: A 35-year-old Small Business Owner

"Committed, strong, and spontaneous, I am true to who I am (Charisms). As I take care of myself, freely speak my mind, and admit I don't know (Stretches), the bright light of my love (Charism) moves us all to live into our higher calling (Impossible Possibility)."

David: event producer

"Whether I am ON or STILL, my authentic presence awakens the human spirit."

A short and sweet GPS. David came across as a positive, motivational, upbeat guy, interested in whomever he was with, but it occasionally seemed forced, like an act, like he was trying to come across as if he cared. The Stretch for him was to let go of having to be ON, practice dropping into the stillness and authentic presence, his Charism. Awakening the human spirit was his Impossible Possibility.

He says this: "One big Aha! for me at my Intensive was realizing how much of the time I was 'on.' Onstage, trying to get people to notice me. What a relief to re-discover that my just *being in the room* has a positive impact on people at a deep level. I knew this in my head—like an idea—but it didn't really live in me. When I catch myself 'on' now, I say my GPS, do a complete breath, and relax. One outcome is that as I have less need to be the center of attention, other people have a greater chance to bring their unique gifts to the agenda. We're getting a richer product out of our meetings with more input from more people!"

Sometimes a GPS turns out to be short:

Jerry: middle manager

"I am enough."

This simple phrase changed his life, allowing him to cease his struggle to 'matter' and strain to be significant to everyone he met.

Betty: school teacher

"Secure & wise, I embrace my fallibility, as I trust my adventurous spirit and nurture the gifts of the next generation."

Steve: consultant

"Present and at peace; as I accept myself and others exactly the way we are, *we* become whole. When I am 'just myself', my passionate energy and gentle heart help *us* come into the fullness of our being. *My flaws reveal my true gifts.*"

Chuck: mortgage lender

"Held in the palm of God's hand, living deeply yet care free, my tough love, self-confidence and spiritual vitality deepen our faith and heals us all. I am your kindred spirit."

(Even though the Intensive is not religious in any way, a large number of GPSs contain spiritual phrases—a testimony, I believe, to what lives down there deep inside each of us when we can peel away the layers and get into the core of who we are.)

Linda: *homemaker*

"I go to the silence to seek God's love and the wisdom of my soul. I revel in who I am, birth that new reality, and become an instrument of light for others."

Jessica: *therapist and life coach*

"Standing in my power, I deliver God's dream. Radiantly gifted, passionate, and perceptive, I allow my spirit to move me. My lyrical grace and loving touch enlivens us all to joyfully be who we are. *I am a light giving life.*"

Over the years, the language of your GPS may shift. (I have had five in the last ten years.) As you step into your Stretches and become more natural with them, they cease to be Stretches, and new ones emerge to capture your attention. Becoming who you are happens in lightning moments, or in a series of gradual morphing moments, but that is our 'assignment' while we are here.

Now that you have greater clarity about what's been running you, about who you are underneath all that 'stuff' and why you are here, the question is, WHAT WILL UNLEASH ME?

Question 5: What will unleash me?

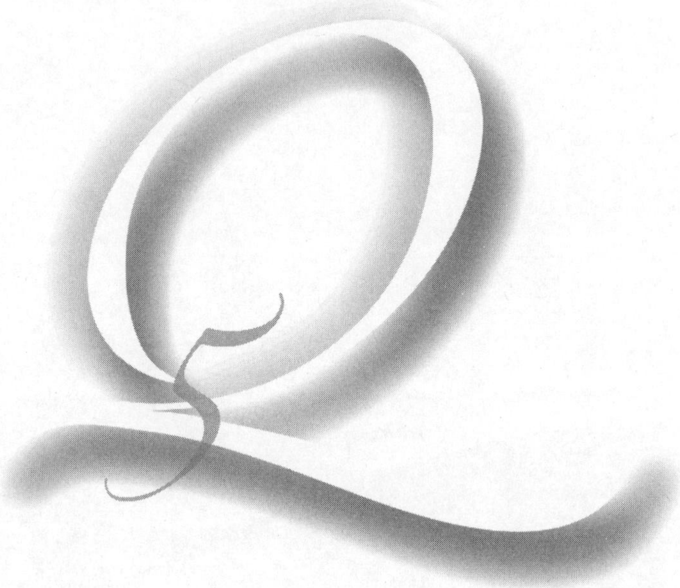

Chapter Twenty

Letting Go and Opening Up

Now that you are conscious of what *confronts* you—inside and out, what you *bring* to each moment, what has been *running* you unconsciously, and what deeply *calls* you, it is time to explore the fifth and final question: WHAT WILL UNLEASH YOU?

How many times have you had a significant 'aha moment' of insight or awareness and told yourself, "This time, it's going to stick! This time I am actually going to follow through." Then, a few months, or weeks, or hours, or even minutes later, you can't find the insight or the commitment anywhere?

What will it take this time to avoid falling into your old pattern? What will you need to DO or BE this time that will ensure a transformation? Remember: transformation is a lot more difficult than simple change. Change can take place inside your current paradigms, but not transformation. Transformation means changing the very paradigms themselves.

Pain And Possibility: The Parents Of Transformation

It has been said that *"Success has many parents, but failure is an orphan."* When it comes to successful transformation, however, the same two partners get things going every time: Pain and Possibility. Both are necessary but not sufficient to generate true transformation. There is one more factor. No deep, lasting change, i.e., *transformation,* can take place—in individuals, groups or larger organizations, regardless of the Pain (or, in its milder form, Discomfort) and Possibility present—without a passage through *Chaos,* the world's birthing center, where transformation comes into being.

Pain: The Father Of Change And Transformation

In this context, I am seeing 'pain' as the awareness of an unacceptable disequilibrium, or a significant discrepancy between the way things *are* and the way they *could or should be.*

As a consultant, therapist, and change facilitator for many years, pain is the only motivator that I trust. Too many times I have seen well-meaning people pursuing a habit-shift get scared at the moment of truth in a change process and revert to the old way. The people who are able to create and sustain fundamental change are usually in the grip of some kind of personal, professional, financial, and/or emotional pain.

This kind of pain manifests itself in various ways. It could be the strain of unresolved conflict with a life partner, close friend or colleague, a breakdown in communication between a spouse and a teenage son, the awareness of some kind of eating or drinking disorder, or even difficulty in choosing a life path. It's that little voice inside that whispers, "This is not working."

Pain by itself, though, is seldom enough. The 'pain' of being overweight, for instance, may or may not lead you to a new body shape. The 'pain' which comes from the realization that a marriage is not working, may or may not result in a breakthrough. Something else is needed.

Possibility: *The Mother Of Transformation*

There is another ingredient in the recipe for transformation. Since pain is awareness of an existing gap between the way things are and the way they could be, the implication is that with the pain comes a *possibility*, something not seen as achievable in the current situation. The overweight person must actually see him/herself as leaner and healthier. The partners in a relationship have to be able to see the crisis turning into breakthrough. The work team or organization must see the possibility of the situation resolved, with productivity at peak levels. Pain moves you to stand in front of the doorway to transformation. Possibility is what moves you to step through that door to what lies on the other side. If you cannot see or imagine a possibility for yourself, you will stand at that doorway, feeling the pain, and not make the move forward.

As I pointed out in exploring Question 2: WHAT ARE YOU BRINGING?, possibility not only provides the direction for change, it also defines the space within which the change occurs. The greater the possibility perceived or allowed, the more likely fundamental, transformative change becomes. Seminar attendees who participate as if their life or job depends on what happens will be more likely to leave transformed than people who show up because the boss sent them. Small possibility, small change. Big possibility, big change.

What Blocks Possibility: The Thermostat

Inside each of us there are conscious and unconscious forces at work in the system which function to maintain what is called *homeostasis*, keeping things the way they are. (From *homeo* = like, and *stasis* = from the verb to stand.) Think of a thermostat. Its job is to regulate the temperature in a room, not letting it get either too hot or too cold, but keeping it within a range that has been pre-set into the thermostat. That's homeostasis: small variations within a narrow range of possibility, in this case, temperature. If you have the thermostat set for 68 degrees, the room temperature can only vary from 67 to 69 degrees before the thermostat kicks the heating or cooling function on or off to regulate the air temperature within its space. It's the same thing happening inside us as human beings. We call this kind of simple change within the paradigm First Order Change. Transformation is Second Order Change.

If you are reading this book, you are probably hoping for Second Order Change, but you also probably want it to happen without having to let go of anything you are attached to, without having to experience discomfort! Second Order Change, or transformation, or breakthrough, takes place only when you get outside the range of the familiar and into new territory. *You cannot produce Second Order Change with a First Order Change mindset.* What doea it take to get you ready for that kind of change? Usually a breakdown of some kind.

The Flat Tire: *Breakdown Or Situation Normal?*

When pain and possibility are both present and acknowledged fully, I call this convergence point in time and space a *breakdown*. Jesse Watson, creative change consultant and colleague, talks about a flat tire as a fitting metaphor for breakdown. "Just having a flat tire on your car doesn't necessarily mean that you're having a breakdown," he says. "You have to be going somewhere!" If your car is sitting in the garage with a flat tire, but hasn't been used for a year, you won't experience the situation as a breakdown.

Breakdown consists of at least two essential components: going somewhere (possibility) and not getting there (pain). In this way, a breakdown is actually quite useful, because it can reveal where you were hoping or intending to go. When I am working with leaders and/or their organizations, and they tell me they and their people are frustrated, I say, "Great! Now maybe you can get somewhere, because frustration is a sign of commitment to some kind of direction or intention." When they tell me there is 'turbulence' in the situation, again I say, "Great! Because turbulence is a sign of possibility. No turbulence, no possibility."

For fundamental change to take place in your life, you must:

1. feel some pain, some turbulence, experience a breakdown of some kind,
2. see and want a new possibility,
3. but not know how to get there,
4. be committed to discovering a new way of thinking, and
5. open up to the possibility of transformation.

'Transformation' is a complete and fundamental change in the basic form of something. It is not a modification of anything that already is. It is bringing into existence something that *was not* a moment before. It is an act of pure creation, *ex nihilo,* 'out of nothing.' This place of nothingness, from which transformation comes, is *chaos.*

Chaos: *The Birth Canal For Transformation*

First order—superficial—change can occur in virtually any situation with very little pain, since it represents a moving around or modification of what is already present. Second order—creative—change or transformation is, by definition, 'impossible.' It represents a bringing forth of something totally new which was not there before, and which could not have been predicted on the basis of what was already there.

For transformation to occur, the existing mental box must fall away like the discarded skin of a molting snake. The current thinking pattern must be broken down. You must find yourself released from the grip of the old context. This leaves you not with a new *pattern*, but with an *empty space* within which a new pattern (creation) can occur. In other words, you must find yourself in a *void*, without any life jacket or props or ideas about how to proceed; with nothing to hold onto, no way to save yourself. In that instant, you are open to what shows up, which could not have shown up as long as you were holding onto anything you thought might work to save you from the experience of being in an empty space, of standing alone in the void.

In The Beginning Was The Void

The creation myths of the world's oldest religions reveal that the ancient ones knew the same basic truth about creation: some kind of emptiness preceded the birth of the cosmos. Several of these myths actually use their word for chaos, the absence of anything familiar or known. For the ancients, the world came out of the unknown, the void.

In the Genesis story about this moment, the one I know the most about, the first few verses are often translated, "And God's spirit moved over the face of the deep." As usual, the translation leaves a lot on the table. The word for spirit here, *ruach*, has to be seen in this context as *the forceful breath of life*, breathing life into what has been created. It's a kind of onomatopoeia: *ruach*, when pronounced forcefully, Roo-Ach! sounds like a sneeze, which captures the sense of air, moving powerfully, like the wind, moving things around. 'Wind' is, in fact, the English word often chosen by translators for *ruach*, as is 'spirit.' Spirit, wind, invisible mover, life-giving force. All connected linguistically in the ancient language. Interesting.

And the verb used for 'moved over' is the same one used elsewhere to describe the actions of a mother eagle hovering over her nest, a scene of maternal love in action. Put all this together, and a much more accurate and powerful translation becomes possible: "And God's loving intention hovered over the void (or chaos)." In other words, what the Creator brought to the party to interact with the chaos, the void, the nothingness, was *a loving intention.*

Chaos was not only the birthing context for the origin of the cosmos, however, it was also seen by the sages to play a central role in bringing about the kind of fundamental change—*conversion, salvation, satori* or *enlightenment*—sought by individual believers. For personal transformation to take place, there also had to exist that space of nothingness or emptiness, that 'dying to be alive' of Judeo/Christian theology, the 'emptying of the mind so that new life can be poured in' of Eastern thought.

As you face the need for transformation in your life, you must bring a loving intention into the chaos and fear that confronts you.

Chaos + loving intention = transformation.

A Scientist's View Of Chaos: *Disequilibrium*

Some years ago Belgian Nobel laureate Ilya Prigogine startled the scientific world with his theories on the thermodynamics of non-equilibrium systems. His colleagues in chemistry were still being influenced by thinking from the Age of the Machine, emphasizing order, predictability, stability, and equilibrium, in a world which was essentially a closed system operating with linear cause and effect relationships. However, Prigogine and his students in the Brussels School were focusing their attention on the *dis*-order, apparent randomness, instability and disequilibrium of non-linear relationships they found in chemical reactions. A central idea he put forward was that new order and new organization can, and often does, *arise spontaneously out of chaos* in systems which are "far from equilibrium" through a process called self-organization.

Prigogine saw that when a molecule's implicate (existing) order starts to fall apart, it faces a moment of choice, a 'bifurcation point.' It can either go out of existence, or reorganize itself at a higher level to accommodate the new variables.

If Prigogine is correct, the potential for transformation is directly proportional to the lack of order present in the structures holding or defining the situation. *The more chaos, the greater the potential for significant change.*

Social scientists have taken Prigogine's work to heart and applied his principles to human systems. The potential for deep change in any social system, from the individual to the largest organization or society, is directly related to the breaking down of those basic concepts which have held things together in the past (homeostasis), and which are now, usually inadvertently, holding back the movement to a higher level of organization. When things look darkest, that's the moment when the system is most open to a new configuration. New order comes out of braving and moving through the emptiness and chaos. Maybe it is true that *'the night is darkest just before the dawn.'*

What a frightening prospect! Does this mean we have to be driven into a world of chaos where all our treasured operating principles crumble in front of us before any kind of fundamental change can take place? If Prigogine and the ancients are right, the answer may be, *"Yes."* Every transformational human being, from Jesus and Buddha, Moses and Mohamed, to Gandhi and Martin Luther King, Jr., has operated from this position: that the current basic concepts must be let go, especially those which have kept us from seeing what was really there, before creative change, innovation or transformation has a chance.

What We Have to Let Go

The good news is that what breaks down is not reality, but our *concept* of reality. It is our *illusions*, which need to be let go of, so that we might see reality uncovered as it really is. It's our current 'map' of the way things are that we have to let go of, not life itself. We end up *feeling* lost and not knowing what to do. The instant we let go of the things we 'know' we can count on, and act as if we do not know, we are open to transformation.

In our day-to-day life, we are pulled so hard by the forces in and around us that it is very hard to step back and let go. How do we move through the illusions of our certainties and move forward into our greater reality as we become more fully who we truly are, unleashing our potential, activating our charisms, expressing our *tov*?

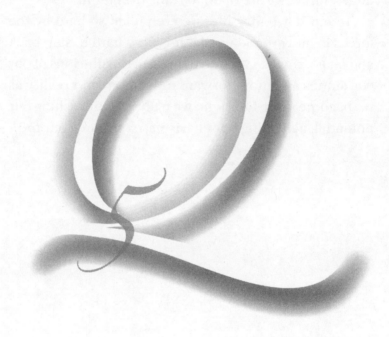

Chapter Twenty-One

Enlarging the Sweet Spot

Remember that Sweet Spot described in Chapter Seventeen—the one where everything is in balance and flow, leaving you feeling effective and fulfilled? Would you be interested in knowing how to increase the size of that Sweet Spot for yourself at home and at work? That's what comes next. I call them The Four Biggies.

The Four Biggies

You can't just grit your teeth and grunt and exert your way into the Sweet Spot. It comes as a by-product of other actions. While the Sweet Spot is *not* within your direct control, the good news is that the actions leading to it *are*. Each of the following Biggies is something well within your control. Put them together and you are in the Sweet Spot of maximum effectiveness and fulfillment—a transformation of major proportions.

Biggie 1:   *The Power Of Presence*
Showing Up for What Happens

Everything begins with your being where you are. How can you be anywhere else? If you are in Miami and want to go to San Francisco, you can't start in Phoenix, just because it happens to be a lot closer to your goal. Your journey in life starts and ends with this moment. It's all you have to work with. Fear is focusing on the future. Anger is focusing on the past. In the present moment there is only whatever IS, without interpretation. The first Biggie, the *sine qua non* (the essential element) of transformation, is to *'show up' for what is happening.*

I use a wonderful exercise to demonstrate the power of presence. One person in a pair begins to tell his partner about some important person or event in his life—while the listener is only twenty-five percent present. This means that seventy-five percent of his attention is somewhere else—anywhere else. Most listeners pick up their cell phone or pretend to be making notes about something, glancing occasionally at their partners and nodding absent-mindedly. After a few moments of such conversation, I stop the process and ask what is happening to the ones trying to tell their story. In every seminar, they report things like, "I lost track of what I was saying;" and, "I couldn't even remember what I was wanting to talk about!" At that, I underline what has happened: The *listener* had the power to disconnect the speaker from himself and his message. "Look how powerful the listener is!" I say.

The former listener in the exercise now gets to be the one speaking, and sets out to tell her partner about her special person or situation—with the partner starting out at 25%. I tell them, "It's Pay-Back!" Then, after a minute or so, I shout the instructions, "Go to a hundred percent! Go to a hundred percent!" Stopping things a few minutes later, I ask the listeners to tell me what they did to bring themselves to one hundred percent. They usually report things like:

- ⋄ make good eye contact.
- ⋄ lean forward, toward the person.
- ⋄ ask questions, interact, don't just sit passively.
- ⋄ turn toward the other person.
- ⋄ put stuff down and focus on the other person.

Then I ask the group, "Have you ever been in an interaction with someone who was doing all these things exactly right—and yet you had the distinct feeling they were actually just running some techniques on you? Like maybe a salesperson or a server in a restaurant who has been to a sales training course?" Then I ask, "What would you say has to be present underneath all those techniques to keep them from just being manipulation?" Eventually, someone will say, "You have to care." It's that simple. I usually underline it: "If you can find some authentic reason to care about the conversation—or about the other person, or about the cause or mission—enough to truly 'show up,' then the techniques will take care of themselves."

Then I challenge the group to reach for what I call 110% presence. That's the internal place you go when you are with a special person, say at a restaurant. You know what I am talking about. It's being so present, so focused, so gently 'there' that a waiter could drop dishes right beside you and you would hardly notice. When the first speaker gets a chance to try again, this time with the listener at 110% presence, the difference is striking—even amazing. People find themselves remembering, thinking and saying things they haven't said or thought in years—or even never. People find themselves getting a little emotional, too. There is usually a profound stillness in the room when I stop the conversation after the 110% presence segment. Something really 'happened' during that exchange. People were moved by the interaction.

Your presence is alchemy: It can turn lead into gold. The reverse is also true: The absence of your presence can turn gold into lead.

If being present is so wonderful and powerful, then why are we reluctant to go there? Because, if we are a hundred and ten percent present, who knows what might happen! It's a lot safer to hang out in the mid-range, half there or mostly there, but keeping one foot on the brake to ensure things don't go too deep. The following chart shows what I mean:

How present are you for interactions?
Where do you tend to operate?

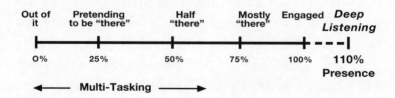

Here's an experiment: Consciously bring yourself 110% present today in every interaction and see what happens—in you, with other people, and to the situation. See whether it doesn't transform your day into a new experience—even with people you have been living or working with for years. Even with people you don't especially like. *Especially* with people you don't especially like.

Try another experiment: Stop multi-tasking! I know you do it all day. The logic runs like this: *If I do three things at the same time, in an 8 hour day, I can get 24 hours worth of work done!* Wrong. Think about it. If you're doing two or three things at the same time, you are missing 50% or 66% of each of the things you are attending to.

Multi-tasking And The Mind

Here's a sobering factoid about your brain from my colleague, Karen Wright: four hundred billion bits of data come into your senses every second, but your brain can only 'notice' or attend to 2,000 bits of that data. The result? You are missing 99.99999995% of everything coming at you—and that's without multi-tasking! Add in multi-tasking and the amount of what you are missing gets downright scary. Something in what you are missing is going to come back to haunt you, I promise. Experiment with focusing on one thing at a time today and watch what happens to your effectiveness and sense of fulfillment. When the people you have inadvertently trained to interrupt you (by responding when they do) try again today, just gently ask them to come back at _____ (give them a specific time) and say something like, "You deserve 110% of my attention and right now I can't give it to you, but I will when you are here at _____."

Biggie 2:   *Authenticity*
Bringing All of Who You Are to Everything You Do

Take a moment to look at the following questions. How would the people who know you best 'grade' you on each of these? How would you grade yourself on each of these?

- ◇ How real are you?
- ◇ Do you ring true to other people?
- ◇ How much of a chameleon are you? (How often do you modify your own reality to appear more pleasing to others?)
- ◇ Can people read you easily—or is it hard for people to know what is happening inside you?
- ◇ Do you walk your talk?

These all get at the question of authenticity. The word comes from the same root (*auto* or self in the Greek) from which we get words like automobile and author. The authenticity question could be summed up this way: What is moving you? Who or what is 'authoring' your moments? Is it you, or someone or something else?

The first ingredient in unleashing yourself is to show up 110%; but that begs the question: Who is it that is showing up? Is it you, or someone else? Remember 'Peeling the Onion' and what was revealed as your 'Con' or 'Autopilot?' When you are being run by that ancient internal navigation system—which is most of the time—you are not being authentic, because you are attempting to be someone you think will get you what you are angling for and avoid what you are terrified of.

Take a look at this mandala. It is actually a graphic used in our Intensives.

On the outer ring is all the stuff you put out there for the world to see and relate to. It's your Persona with all its gifts and concerns about looking good and staying safe. It's your automatic self, the one you hope will work.

Just inside that ring of the mandala is your Shadow, that darker aspect of who you are—or are afraid you might be. It's where your Terror (being rejected, abandoned, hated, etc.) lives, which makes it impossible to access the life transforming gifts of your Stretches that also reside there.

Then, way down in the center of the mandala is an interesting image. Can you see the three intersecting circles? That's where The Sweet Spot lives. Where *tov* lives. Where your spirit lives with your unique charism. Think of that space down in the very center as your authentic self, the real you, your essence, your soul. That is the You who is not addicted or afraid, who is beyond the many games of life, and who is capable of simply being who and what you are. When you are thinking, this is who is listening. It is the You who is not at the effect of all the drama your mind makes up about what is happening. When you 'notice what you notice' this is who or what is doing the noticing.

See the thumb print there? That's you in all your uniqueness. There is not another one like you on the earth—never has been and never will be.

For anyone reading this and starting to get antsy about all this talk about the Self, and YOU and how unique you are, let me remind you of a great saying I heard many years ago as a summary of the creation story in Genesis, the first book of the Hebrew Scriptures and the Christian Bible. The other creation story in there, not the one about The Fall that has humans being lost and evil. The one that says humans are "a little lower than the angels" and that we are the Creator's partners in co-creating this world. That one. You may have heard the saying: God don't make no junk.

The denial of the Self that has permeated the conservative Christian tradition has become a kind of inverted egotism. Jesus, Buddha, Moses, Mohammed, all had strong senses of Self. They knew who they were and had the courage to just be that. They didn't deny their gifts; they used them.

As Question 4: WHAT CALLS ME? suggests—Whom or what do I put my Self in the service of? Where do I aim all these gifts I have been given? Am I protecting my self-concept, that illusionary self I am seeking to maintain, or am I willing to let that little self die in order to unleash that greater Self for fuller and freer service to self, others, and life itself?

Practicing greater authenticity does not mean just blurting whatever comes into your mind or heart. However, it does mean having the freedom and the courage to do that if you choose to. It means knowing who you are, and having the courage to be exactly that, no more, and—also importantly—no less. Like the soil, humus, it just is what it is. Ready for whatever comes along.

Biggie 3: A Spirit Of Inquiry
Learning from Whatever Happens

Here's another Pop Quiz. How would the people who know you best see you on these:

- Do you see interactions as debates to be won or points to be made?
- Do you argue about the rightness of your position before understanding what the other people are saying?
- How willing are you to learn—especially about things you already know?
- How open are you to having your perspective changed?
- How hard or costly is it for people to give you feedback?

⋄   Can you hold negative situations and experiences as *exactly* what is needed and, on reflection, see them as contributions to your development?

Biggie 3 is actually what the whole book is about: learning to learn from experience. This way of living requires an emotional investment in something— something you are so eager to learn you can't wait to get into it. Remember a time when you felt like that? Maybe it was in a classroom setting (maybe not), maybe a strong desire to learn to play a sport or a musical instrument. I can still picture the scene on the Collegiate School playground in Richmond, Virginia, when I was eleven or twelve years old, and trying to learn to shoot a jump shot. I stood there, sometimes with a buddy or two, and shot and shot and shot at that basket, missing, stumbling, awkward, frustrated, but eventually successful. That feeling of *'Yes!'* is still within me. It represents a moment of learning a new skill that began with an almost overpowering spirit of inquiry. I simply wasn't going to quit trying until I mastered that shot.

What is something you don't know how to do and have an almost overpowering urge to master? Start there.

Biggie 4:   *Go For Tov*
Fully Expressing Who You Are
Tov is discussed at length in Chapter Sixteen, as part of WHAT CALLS ME?, but arises again here because *tov* is what happens when you *unleash* your charism into the world, the best of who you are, out there where the world can see it.

How To Recognize The Tov State

I know I am in the *tov* state when I am:

- ⬦   physically balanced and stable.
- ⬦   breathing deeply from my belly.
- ⬦   relaxed, calm, and focused.
- ⬦   aware of what is happening, internally and externally.
- ⬦   appreciative of myself and others.
- ⬦   feeling my emotions–and learning from them.
- ⬦   compassionate and connected to others and to my environment.
- ⬦   able to receive and give sincere acknowledgement.
- ⬦   energized by a higher purpose.
- ⬦   unattached to the outcome of a situation.
- ⬦   experiencing joy and laughing often.
- ⬦   bigger than my challenges.

I am in tov when I bring a sense of peace, security, and accomplishment to my actions, so that what I DO is an expression or manifestation of who I AM. The world will give me feedback, and it will be interesting, even meaningful, but not addictive—not the main reason for what I am doing.

The GPS Practice

We'll come back to it, but the practice for making your GPS (Greater Purpose Statement) useful is simple. It involves catching yourself when you are 'hooked' (emotionally reactive to something that has happened) and then stopping, taking at least one complete breath, and centering into a word or phrase from your GPS (discussed on Page 260). For me, it's often my bullion cube: *I am a spiritual warrior.* That is usually enough to help me get unhooked, and reclaim my center of courageous authenticity and compassionate insight, looking for what will unleash the human spirit.

Q

Chapter Twenty-two

From Automatic to Authentic Living

Now you possess all the tools you need to make the shift:

⋄ You have a handle on your Con, and the Somebody Training that created it.

⋄ You know what is driving your daily default game—your Addiction and your Terror.

⋄ You know at least several Stretches from your Shadow you need to step into to take your life to the next level of purpose, power, and peace.

⋄ You have your GPS (Greater Purpose Statement). What you need now is a method, a path you can take whenever you want to.

Remember, I asked you when is a good time to catch yourself in your Con? Now ... now ... now ... now ... It's always running. Making it stop altogether is the Advanced Class. All you really need to be able to do is 'catch yourself in the act' (operating in your Con), and gently and gracefully step away and into your GPS and your Shadow Stretches.

Let's start with the one we know the best—Automatic Living. Then you will add Authentic Living to the mix, and keep them together in your heart and mind. We all go back and forth between them all the time, usually (before we wake up) unconsciously. People who are mastering Authentic Living simply catch themselves in their act faster and get off it sooner—and with little or no self blame. Note that the goal of Automatic Living is looking good and staying safe, and the method is manipulating self, others, and life. Great way to live, isn't it? I'll walk you through mine to give you an idea how it works.

As shown at the conclusion of Question 3, mine would go like this: Hello, I'm presenting myself as *The Eagle Scout* who is *bright, resourceful, clever, helpful, alive, and compassionate*, and trying hard not to be seen as Bobby Knight, who is *emotionally out of control, has to be right, and is driven to win*, but it's all in the service of my hidden agenda, which is angling to get hits of being *adored, wanted, and mattering*, and avoid any possible hint of being *dumped, replaced, or not mattering*.

Hello, I'm presenting myself as the	and trying hard NOT to be seen as
Eagle Scout	Bobby Knight
who is	**who is**
Bright & quick	Emotionally out of control
Courageous & compassionate	Has to be right
Vital & alive	Driven to win at any cost
Transformational	

get continuous 'hits' of being (my Addiction)	and avoid any possible hint of being (my Terror) who is
Adored, truly wanted, and respected	Dumped, or replaced, or not mattering

Being In Your Own Movie

These boxes are very powerful if you let yourself go with it. Imagine that you are writing a movie script with an Eagle Scout as the central character. In order for him to 'stay in role' (being helpful, clever, resourceful, compassionate, etc), what kind of people and situations would you need to write into the script? (Here's an interesting question: what kind of people would you *not* write into the script—because it might force him out of his comfortable Eagle Scout role? What about *other* Eagle Scouts?)

✦ For the Eagle Scout to be helpful, you'd need to write in people who need his help.

✦ You'd need to have people in it who weren't quite as resourceful, to give him a chance to shine.

✦ For him to find opportunities to be clever, he'd have to be around people and situations that demanded fast action to solve a tough problem.

✦ A compassionate Eagle Scout requires needy people around to stay 'in role.'

Get it? (Given that Con, can you see how it's no wonder that over the years I have made a life out of being a therapist, conflict consultant, and organization transformation consultant?)

As long as I am unaware, and don't know about my Con (being The Eagle Scout), when I walk into a room, I am automatically scanning for where my clever, resourceful, bright compassion will be needed, and I focus my attention there. Like the carpet expert from Chapter Four, I am noticing what I am trained to notice, and will gravitate toward those people and situations where I can stay in role. This becomes truly important when I realize that, like the carpet expert, I am missing anything that doesn't fit into my movie—like: who does *not* need help, or how are things working just fine, or look at all the *other* clever, resourceful people in the room.

Work/Life As A Continuous Casting Call

The key thing to get is that when you are in your Con, *you are forcing people to take a role in your movie*. That's Automatic Living. When you are not aware of what you are doing, people will simply show up for you as a character that fits into your script—or not. The ones that don't fit usually don't make the final cast in your movie. You will find yourself not being around them much, and/or making them wrong in a way that justifies your ignoring them. It's as if you are in a continuous Casting Call, looking for people to take a role in your movie. Hey, it's what passes for life for many, many people. Taking on the FIVE QUESTIONS breaks the pattern and will not allow you to run your Con any longer without realizing what you are doing. It's a bummer, actually. Ignorance *is* bliss.

Shifting Your State

Whenever you catch yourself in your Con (now ... now ... now ...) you need to shift your state. We go through many states off and on all day long. Happy, sad, confident, scared, angry, pushy, retiring, vulnerable, conscious, unconscious, etc. Every one of those states has a certain physical, emotional, and psychological shape to it.

Let me illustrate this with an exercise developed by my friend and colleague, Ted Buffington. Imagine that you just won the Gold Medal in an Olympic event, running faster than every other runner in the world. Now imagine that you are up on the stand, waving to the cheering crowd, proud of what you have accomplished for your country and for yourself. The national anthem starts to play. Picture yourself there. Get into the stance you would be in. Just put the book down and stand the way you'd be standing, feeling the way you'd be feeling. What would be going on in your body (hands, feet, back, chest, tummy, legs, face)?

Okay, got that? Now, *without changing your physical stance,* try to feel depressed.

It can't be done. You will have to shift something in your physical stance to get into that depressed mood.

Now, reverse it. Get into a position that is you feeling completely dejected, lost, depressed. Think of a situation where you are completely hopeless and helpless. Got it?

Hold that stance and, without changing your physical stance, try to feel empowered or hopeful. Tough, isn't it? It can't be done. You will have to shift something in your *physical* state to get into that victorious *emotional* state.

You may not be able to recognize it right away, but you have a familiar stance and state associated with your Con. Do you know someone who looks as if they're carrying the weight of the world on their shoulders? Or anyone who always has to be right and in control? Or someone who expects to be attacked at any time? Each of those automatic, default ways of being (their Cons) looks a certain way on them, physically.   Yours does, too. It may be too subtle for you to notice, but I guarantee, it's there, and some people close to you know what it looks like. Something in your tone of voice, a gesture, the way you carry your head, or walk. Look closely and you may see the clues of your Con embedded in your body. Ask someone who knows you well to 'mirror you' and/or tell you what they notice when you're just being normal, and be prepared to be surprised. That internal state, that cluster of physical, emotional, and psychological elements can and will shift as you become more adept at catching yourself in your Con and moving into your GPS.

While in your Con, you may begin to be aware of how you are angling for your Addiction, setting people up to give you what you think you need. You may catch yourself subtly manipulating people, putting all your amazing Persona gifts in the service of looking good and staying safe.

When you gently pull away from your Con and put all your Persona gifts—*and* your Shadow Stretches—in the service of your GPS, a very different state shows up.

We can see it the moment it happens in the seminar. Someone's face will soften, or they will sit straighter in their chair, or their voice will change. It's often truly amazing to see. Everyone in the room can notice it. It's not just that they are having a different thought, *they are in a completely different state of being.*

Making The Shift

Picture yourself moving from page to page, from left to right, from Automatic to Authentic Living. I like to think of it like this:

When I catch myself in my Con, I choose to:

⬦ STOP
⬦ BREATHE
⬦ DROP IN

Stop, Breathe, Drop In

To snap out of the trance of our normal way of operating—our Con—we need to create a little break in the flow of what is happening. The breath is one of the best tools for managing our consciousness we have available. My Yoga Master taught me, "The breath is the leash (or the harness) for the mind." Since the state we are in is a result of the pattern of thoughts, frequently old and out-of-date, we need to wedge out a space in our minds for a new thought pattern to have a chance.

It's pretty simple, actually. Athletes, singers, actors, martial artists, public speakers, anyone facing difficult situations naturally learns to do this. It results in amazingly powerful, yet completely relaxed focus, making you more ready for whatever is in front of you.

- Look off into the middle distance.

- Soften your gaze. (Don't focus on anything.)

- Exhale completely, squeezing out all the stale air.

- Inhale slowly and deeply, filling the entire lung capacity.

- Hold the breath for a count of five.

- While you are holding, bring to your mind a phrase from your GPS, or a Stretch you intend to practice immediately, or your So That/ Impossible Possibility.

- Gently exhale, and, if you are free to do so, do it with a deep sigh.

- Do whatever is next from this rejuvenated place.

Want a perfect example? Watch Seattle Mariner's All-Everything baseball outfielder, Ichiro Suzuki. As he steps up to the plate, he goes through a set routine, kneeling and stretching and pointing his bat at the pitcher. Watch his breath. He takes three distinct breaths during the flow, always at the same time. When he's done, he is ready, focused, laser-like in his relaxed intensity. I am convinced that his breathing routine is a major factor in his leading the league as a hitter year after year.

Notice that when you make this shift from Automatic Living to Authentic Living, you get to bring along everything that is worthwhile from your Con. All those highly developed skills and techniques that are truly present in your Persona come along. That means stepping into what your Shadow Character has to teach you, as well as consciously practicing the Stretches you identified in Chapter Eleven. As I said at the beginning of this book, you do *not* have to *change* yourself and become someone else—you need to *become* your self, even more fully. You need to bring all of who you ARE, The Good, The Bad, and The Ugly, to everything you DO. At first, you may feel a little funny, a little vulnerable, a little raw or unpolished. This is a good thing. It means you are no longer operating inside the comfortable and predictable zone of your Autopilot or Con and its clever manipulations. It means that something brand new is about to happen—not more of the same.

Going Authentic

Let's now see how Authentic Living looks, compared with Automatic Living. Here's mine.

As I make this shift, I bring everything in my Persona	and these Stretches from my Shadow:
Bright & quick Courageous & compassionate Vital & alive Transformational	Expressing my upsets sooner Going all out for I 'see' Valuing the validity of my work Being clear about my needs

As I do this, I still 'run the risk' of being

Adored, truly wanted and Respected	and	Dumped, replaced or not mattering

BUT WHO CARES?

Now fill in the form for yourself, using the tools you've just acquired.

Creeping Awareness

Some people who take on this inner work report having developed the capacity to catch themselves in the act, but then they beat up on themselves: "There, I did it again!"

Just relax. This is natural. This is called practice, not instant mastery. You are shifting a lifetime of habitual patterns, but if you stay with it, you will start to experience what I call Creeping Awareness. At first, you will catch yourself some time after an event or 'moment.' It could be the next day—or even the next week. "Oh, man, I sure messed up that time. I fell into my Con and am just now realizing that I was doing it again." You would be able, I am sure, to look back in your life and find hundreds or even thousands of moments where you were operating in your Con. That's catching yourself in the act a long time after the fact.

The next time, though, you may catch yourself *right afterward.* You say or do something and immediately you catch the faint aroma of your Con at work. When that happens, you could actually say something like, "I didn't like where I was coming from just then, and I'd really like to receive what you are telling me. Could we start this conversation again?"

Then, as you practice, you can start to catch yourself *in the Con moment* itself. "Hey, I'm 'hooked' again, and we need to start over. Can we?"

Finally, you can get to the point where you sense the urge to respond to someone from your Con *beforehand.* That's the graduation exercise—catching yourself *before you speak* and dropping into your GPS and your Shadow Stretches as you engage the other person, shifting from Automatic to Authentic.

It has been a great joy to bring this to you. You have no idea how *tov* this whole process has been for me, from beginning to end—even in the times when 'nothing was coming' and during the editing process. I invite you to take on these Five Questions and make them a part of your everyday experience. Put them on your fridge, make your GPS into a screensaver, put your Stretches on a wallet card and look at them from time to time. 'Catching yourself in the act' will become faster and faster. Practice, practice, practice.

Transformation is an ongoing process. We are continually becoming more and more of who we truly are. You'll be amazed. It's a wonderful thing.

Acknowledgments

Who helped make this book happen?

'Birthing' a book is one of the most team-oriented tasks anyone can tackle. Many people played key roles in helping bring this baby into the world, and I am grateful to them all.

Since they first did the Leadership Development Intensive (LDI), on which The FIVE QUESTIONS is based, **Vicki Carter** and **Kathy Davis** have been 'poster children' for the inner work described here. Thank you, Vicki, Kathy, and **Jean Ogilvie**, for the prodding, challenging, encouraging—even cooking—you did to help bring it into being. It would not have happened without you.

The typical executive and his or her organization is often not particularly interested in approaching work as a spiritual practice, but in 1987 **Izaak van Melle**, former CEO of the Dutch company that makes Mentos mints, was such a leader. He had the intuitive courage to ask me if I would work with one of his key executives, **Bert van Dijk**. He said, "John, I want you to do whatever you are moved to do to assist Bert in becoming the leader he is capable of being." What a life-changing invitation—for Bert, and for me! Kudos to you, Bert, the very first Intensive graduate, for proving that four days alone with a facilitator team can transform a life, and for paving the way for the other van Melle leaders who came from all over the world to experience this strange, body-mind-spirit approach. Thank you, **Caroline Dell'uomo**, for bringing us together.

Thanks also to **Bill McKendree**, an AEtna senior Organization Effectiveness leader and early graduate, who finally convinced me in 1987: "It's a program, John!" As a result of Bill's unswerving initiative, (along with AEtna colleagues **Carol Rady** and **Bob Heslin**), the company sent over 100 key leaders and their life partners through the early solo version of the Intensive, launching it for real.

To **Earl Goode** and **Clare Coxey** two senior GTE executives, who trusted my colleague, **Jeananne Oliphant**, enough to bring me in to work with leaders of that huge company, sending their key people through the program over a three-year period.

To my **Gestalt therapy clients** and growth group participants from the 1970s and 1980s with whom I grew up as a practitioner of this kind of deep work.

To many gifted and delightful colleagues, who shaped and improved these concepts with each Intensive they led, in chronological order, from 1987 to the present: **Daya Scherer, Menka Macleod, Catharine Scherer, Barbara Baumgarten, Dan Baumgarten, Ally Rubin, Tricia (Malti) Karpfen, Nick Wolfson, Chandra Smith, Mark Yeoell, Terry Rogers, Bob Kamm, Ingrid Richter, Lynnea Brinkerhoff, Ellen Stapenhorst, Montse Auso, Robyn Wynne-Lewis, Dominic Cirincione, Susan Briehl, Kathy Davis, Noushin Bayat, Maria Kolodziejczyk,** and **Dorota Zawadzka.**

To each of the several thousand men and women leaders, managers (and just regular people) from at least 22 countries who have participated in LDI and associated seminars, for keeping the developmental work going in your own lives and organizations—and for inspiring me and my colleagues with your courage in going back to work and 'facing your tigers.'

To **Bob Crosby** for the 1973 invitation into the work of transforming lives, and creating the 'laboratory' where I could develop the concepts laid out here.

To **Jan Smith**, my own personal development coach for many years, for teaching me the initially painful distinction: *doing* authenticity.

To my early mentors in the work of transformation: **Austin Shell, Fritz Perls, Ron Lippitt, Herb Shepard, Jack Sherwood, Flo**

Hoylman, Ron Short, John Adams, and Juanita Brown.

To Mike Murray, Art McNeil, Ron Short, Dick Finch, Barbara Arney, Bill Yon, John Adams, Stanley Krippner, Doug Henck, Marilyn Neal, H. George Anderson, Kelly Chatman, Dave Myer, Bill Allen, Mike Stephen, Tor Dahl, Ken Blanchard, Carol Orsborn, Martin Rutte, Geoff Bellman, Marv Weisbord, Bill Hawley, Levis Madore, Byrd Ball, Wayne Woodson, John Morrow, Shawna Eldredge, Peter Vaill, Roland Sullivan, Kakuta Hamisi, Chris Henderson, Susan Burchfield, and many other friends and colleagues who have provided encouragement, conceptual input, and a truing-up mechanism over the years.

To Toni Dianne Holm, Publisher extraordinaire, and her creative team: George Edward Tice, *Managing Editor and CFO*; Laura Daniel, *Copy Editor*; David Dalton, *Art Director, onedesign*; and Brenda Thompson, *Editorial Assistant*, who shepherded *Five Questions* from rough draft to finished product. Toni, you are a gift to this world. Thank you! David, I love the book cover! Thank you all for your support.

Finally to my family (Catharine, Jay & Lizanne, David & Carolyn, Asa, and Emma), who have endured and even embraced these concepts in hundreds of 'kitchen counter conversations,' and who, although now scattered, are still the emotional and spiritual base from which my work has been able to go out into the world.

Letter to the Reader

When the idea of writing this book came to me two years ago, it virtually burst out of my heart and mind in a rush, the material coming so rapidly that I couldn't write fast enough. (My mother, a magazine editor, typed 120 words a minute—on a manual typewriter! My father, a newspaperman, typed with two fingers and maybe got to 25-30 words a minute. Unfortunately, I took after Pop in this regard.)

The material came to me in bursts of energy, not well-formed words and phrases, as if it were in a hurry to get here and didn't want to take the time to get formal. It was if I were standing under a fire hydrant, attempting to capture some of the flow as it washed over me. Think of having a dream, a dream that comes with force and insistence. Fragile, yet powerful. Ephemeral, yet solid. Clear one moment, then gone in a flash.

As the wisps of energy got clumsily converted into words, I did my best to retain the power and clarity they had in their less concrete form. They worked their way through my fingers, tickling the keyboard as fast as I could go, and became available to you, the reader. I hope you have caught some of the truth and value that I did as it passed through on its way to you. If you did not, it is my responsibility, and means I must have not done an adequate job of moving it through to you. If you did find it powerful, then you must have been able to enter into a similar state of receptivity.

Now the responsibility passes on to you. There's a story about an old preacher who told his flock, "If you tell me at the door after the service 'That was a great sermon, Pastor!' I am going to say, 'We'll see. We'll see.'" So, if you are sitting there thinking this has been a pretty good book, I say to you, "We'll see. We'll see."

Do something with this material. Think about it. Practice living into The FIVE QUESTIONS. Talk about it with friends and colleagues at work. Read it again and again. Start a book club and discuss it. Send me feedback. I will do my best to respond to each one. Send your comments and questions to me at John. Scherer@SchererCenter.com.

It has been a delight to bring this to you! May our paths cross again.

The Author

John J. Scherer is widely acknowledged by both peers and clients as a pioneer in recognizing the role, and nurturing the growth, of the human spirit in the workplace environment, though the reach of his teachings extends into all areas of life. His mission is *transforming the world at work*™ by *unleashing the human spirit*—starting with his own. Stephen Covey's organization, FranklinCovey, recently named John one of America's Top 100 Thought Leaders in Personal and Leadership Development, along with other notables such as Wayne Dyer, Mark Victor Hansen, and Oprah Winfrey. In addition to his 1993 book *Work and the Human Spirit*, John has written hundreds of articles on leadership and change and has contributed to many books including two chapters in *Chicken Soup for the Soul at Work* and two in *Practicing Organization Development*, considered the 'bible' in this field.

Born and raised in Virginia, John excelled in both sports and academics. He took honors degrees in History and Philosophy from Roanoke College where he won awards recognizing his leadership as well. He went on to US Navy Officer Candidate School and served as Combat Officer on the Destroyer USS EATON, in the 2nd and 6th Fleets, receiving a variety of commendations. Following his tour of duty, he trained in ministry at the Lutheran Seminary in Columbia, South Carolina, again graduating with honors. His first ministry was on the streets with 'people of the night' in Norfolk, Virginia, and then as Lutheran Chaplain at Cornell University in Ithaca, New York. While there, he began his counseling practice as a Gestalt Therapist and Family Counselor. He soon developed a reputation as a facilitator of conflict and change, and business and government leaders began to call on him to resolve difficult issues.

In 1973, John relocated to the Pacific Northwest, where he co-created the nation's first graduate degree in Applied Behavioral Science at Whitworth College, equipping men and women from around the world to become 'change artists.' It was here that he began extending his work internationally as a consultant, speaker, seminar leader, and author.

In 1984, he began a private consultancy which has grown through several stages to become the Scherer Leadership Center (SLC), serving a vast array of clients from both the public and private sectors. Many have sent their 'fast-trackers' through his training programs and high-performance coaching. Since 1987, business and government leaders, both men and women, from more than twenty-two nations have graduated from John's Executive Development Intensive and its companion course, the Leadership Development Intensive, helping them to achieve greater purpose, power and peace. SLC has grown into an international consortium of experienced consultants, coaches, change facilitators and leadership development specialists committed to unleashing the human spirit at work, helping clients design and deliver people-oriented strategies that achieve organizational objectives. SLC has Senior Associates across the USA as well as in Canada, Europe, and the Pacific Rim. All are equipped to deliver world-class developmental experiences, coaching and consulting to large and small organizations and their leaders in Spanish, French, German, Italian, Portuguese, Sicilian,

Farsi, Arabic, and Japanese as well as English.

In 2004, while in Spain facilitating small groups of spiritual leaders at the Parliament of World Religions, John and two colleagues founded Acacia Tree, a non-profit organization whose purpose is to take small groups of organizational leaders to developing countries to work side-by-side with local people on some life-saving project (e.g. digging a well) and reflect in the evenings on what is being learned about leadership and life. The inaugural trip of Acacia Tree was to Kenya in June 2005.

John is a Member of the World Business Academy, the Organization Development Network, The International Organization Development Network, and is an Advisory Board Member of The Mark Victor Hansen Foundation. He lives in Seattle, Washington, plays the guitar, runs or swims and does yoga daily, performs the occasional magic show, and loves to read a good spy novel.

More Applause . . .

"After working alongside John and benefiting from his work for the last ten years, I can honestly say that his book, like his life, packs a real life-changing punch with a velvet glove!"

— Lynnea Brinkerhoff, Center for Human Resource Development and Leadership Studies, University of New Haven

"In this powerful book, John Scherer takes us beyond the everyday race to fix, change, and improve ourselves to a focus and methodology that will actually enable us to live the life our hearts and souls are craving."

— Dwight R. Frindt, Co-Founder, 2130 Partners

"Your materials are an invaluable and rich resource which I draw on all the time to design practices and mini-lessons for my coaching clients. They love the clarity and depth of insight that comes out of your thought exercises, observations and insights."

—Jean Ogilvie, Coach and Organization Development Consultant

"My handwriting is all over the book's pages . . . asking myself, is there something I can do now, anonymously... that three generations from now people will benefit from? Oh, my! You opened up a window full of light and possibility. For the first time I am wondering what seeds I have planted during my passage here."

—Monique Renaud-Gagne

"I learn something worthwhile in every conversation with John. His book is the real deal."

—Lisa Noji, Salon Divas, Seattle, WA

"John Scherer's writing reflects the kind of wisdom won, or perhaps gifted, by a life lived in courage, openness, and service. Come to his table. Share in the feast. Bring your warrior heart."

–Elizabeth Kanada Gorla, Leadership & Personal Development Coach, BC, Canada

"John Scherer's *Five Questions* sets a new standard of excellence for the impact of spirituality in our lives. This magnificent book is a fitting tribute to. his life and work. He's a wonderful friend and role model."

–Michael Stephen, Chairman, Aetna International, Inc. (Retired)

"I prescribe it! Drop in and join this gifted and committed teacher. John's book provides you with an opportunity to engage in one of the more interesting and important journeys you will ever have the pleasure to undertake."

–Bruce Cutter, M.D., Cancer Care Northwest

"John's metaphors are inspired. His words are simple enough to be easily understood, yet deep enough to be profound. This wonderful work fits all levels of people. Like an art, some see colors, some see shapes, and some appreciate age. You will find what you are looking for in this book."

–Dr. Lee Lu, Adjunct Professor, Benedictine University

"Seriously taking on John's *Five Questions* will perform magic in your life–making it a gift to yourself and making you more of a gift to those you care about."

–Mike Murray, President, Creative Interchange Consultants International

"Those of us who know John Scherer are not surprised that the *Five Questions That Change Everything* are not intended to be answered. Rather they describe a way of being that leads readers to the mystery, depth, and greatness of their own lives. This is not a book of good advice, but an announcement of good news to everyone who accepts the challenge to ask these questions."

–William Lesher, Lutheran School of Theology, Chicago

"John has played an instrumental role in the management training for my company. His book gets to the root of any problem, helping you find your own answers. Part trainer, part pastor, and part guru, John is a shining light for all to see."

–Rick Hosmer, Klundt & Hosmer Design Associates

"This book gives you that 'Ah-Hah!' – the sudden startling, BIG insight that makes you shiver; the kind John's clients get in person."

–Dave Myer, former EVP, ACE Hardware

"In my view John is a genius when it comes to personal, professional, and organizational development.

–Robyn Wynne-Lewis, Core Consulting, Leadership Development Specialists, New Zealand

"John cares for the individual. His passion for what he does is remarkable. He shows you your world like you have never seen it before and helps unleash the human spirit, making you a better leader."

–Anupam Narayan - CEO, Red Lion Hotels Corporation

"The real assignment in what John calls 'The Workplace School of Life' is to discover, become and express who you truly are. There is 'homework' offered in *Five Questions*, but it is work that takes you home to who you truly are, making this challenge stunningly easy."

–Domien van Gool, Founder, Leader Academy of Europe, Brasschaat, Belgium

"John Scherer is a gifted consultant and teacher. His deep questions empowered our team to focus, think, plan and act out of our deep purpose. He has the unique ability to help us develop and use our 'compass' to navigate the demands and challenges before and within us."

–Red Burchfield – Evangelical Outreach Mission Director

"Organizations are essentially a group of people in relationships. *Five Questions* helps you make conscious choices about the key principles that guide your life, and thus guide you to a higher level of leadership, performance and self-fulfillment. This is a remarkable book of insights and wisdom.

–Cam Strong – Healthcare Executive, Consultant & Executive Coach - Seattle Washington

"I've been the recipient of John's guidance for over a decade. It has helped me merge companies, work through my true self, and take my personal life to new heights. This book is as transformative as it sounds."

–Ingvar Petursson - Technology Executive

"John's work evokes the self awareness and discovery that each of us has waited for all of our lives. His book is about revelations. It's a must read."

  –Dominic Cirincione- President, Organizational Fitness Associates, Los Angeles

"John reminds us that what happens at work can serve as vital 'lessons' for our personal development. His *Five Questions* empower and inspire. They are valuable principles that will transform your life."

  –Carol Orsborn, Ph.D., author, The Art of Resilience and How Would Confucius Ask for a Raise?

"In this book John Scherer guides us on a path, interweaving the world of business and the realm of spirit, asking us to name what is common: courage, consciousness, and creativity."

  –Mark Kelso, Muddy Angel Music

"What I got out of John's message was, 'Wake up! God isn't through with you yet.' Answering his *Five Questions* can change everything. This book gets my high five!"

  –Art McNeil, author, Leadership: The "I" of the Hurricane - Creating Corporate Energy

"John Scherer belongs to that great tradition of elders who teach through powerful questions. There are few, if any, who can equal him in our times."

  –Bob Kamm, author, Lyric Heart

Further Resources:

The Five Questions That Change Everything
Workbook-based process:

Taking It to the Next Level

To apply The Five Questions, go to

www.the5questions.com

A Workbook-based process for an Armchair Workshop!

. . . . .

**The Five Questions That Change Everything
Weekend Workshop:**

For a schedule or to apply, go to

www.SchererCenter.com

. . . . .

John Scherer and The Scherer Center:

For more information about the author and about
The Scherer Center's consulting work in transforming
global leaders and their organizations, go to:

www.SchererCenter.com